Sam Llewellyn was born on Tresco.
He has written many novels for adults and children,
including three based on Scilly.
This book is the product of his curiosity about the
life, times and motives of earlier generations of
Scillonians and particularly of Augustus Smith,
his great-great uncle.

FOLLOWING PAGES
Looking eastwards from Tresco.

EMPEROR SMITH

The Man Who Built Scilly

SAM LLEWELLYN

THE DOVECOTE PRESS

The mackerel fleet leaving St Mary's.

First published in 2005 by The Dovecote Press Ltd
Stanbridge, Wimborne Minster, Dorset BH21 4JD

Casebound ISBN 1 904349 37 4
Paperback ISBN 1 904359 18 8

Text © Sam Llewellyn 2005

Sam Llewellyn has asserted his rights under the Copyright, Designs
and Patent Act 1988 to be identified as author of this work

Designed by The Dovecote Press
Printed and bound in Singapore

All papers used by The Dovecote Press are natural, recyclable products
made from wood grown in sustainable, well-managed forests

A CIP catalogue record for this book is available
from the British Library

All rights reserved

1 3 5 7 9 8 6 4 2

Contents

Foreword   7

Prologue   8

Wild but Useful   13

Mr Smith Grasps the Nettle   24

The Fortunate Isles   39

The Golden Age   57

Emperor Smith   76

The Emperor at Rest   97

Acknowledgements   101

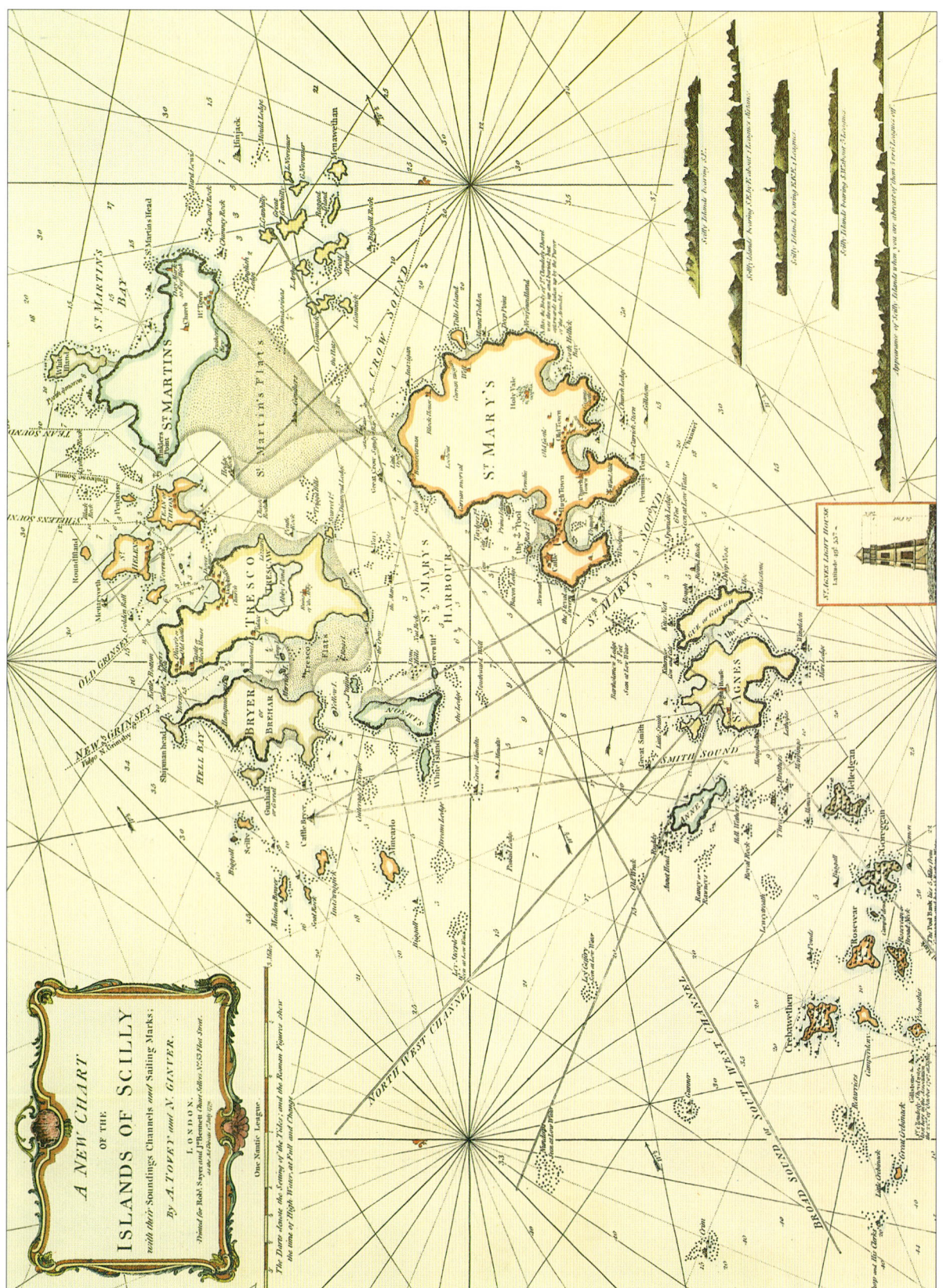

Foreword

ROBERT DORRIEN SMITH

Over the years, there have been numerous articles, books, and pamphlets published about life on Scilly during the nineteenth century, and the influence that Augustus Smith brought to bear. But none of them has been written by an author with such an intimate knowledge of Scilly. Sam Llewellyn was born on Tresco, has written widely about Scilly and its past, and has a natural sympathy for Augustus Smith's character that brings him vividly to life.

Interestingly, Sam Llewellyn has chosen to focus on the man himself and the thought processes that brought Augustus Smith to these islands. As a descendant, I find this fascinating and illuminating. His battles with bureaucrats and courtiers in particular bring a sense of déjà vu.

Sam has also been able to draw on a large amount of unpublished material, including early photographs and Augustus Smith's personal diaries and correspondence. But perhaps the book's greatest pleasure are its watercolours and drawings, some the work of unknown Victorian visitors to Tresco Abbey, others by our mutual ancestors, Fanny le Marchant and Sophia Tower. None has ever been reproduced before – few have ever seen the light of day – so that their colours are as rich and fresh as when they were first finished. Taken together, they breathe new life into the world which Augustus Smith so energetically bestrode, providing a wonderful accompaniment to a book that will delight all lovers of Scilly.

Prologue

THE SALOON of the packet boat *Lord Wellington* was not a place to be confused with the stern cabin of the *Victory*. The *Lord Wellington* was a sailing cutter, fat, slow and decrepit. As Penzance fell astern, the spar-and-barrel Runnel stone buoy crawled by to starboard. Beyond the doubtful varnish of the *Lord Wellington*'s bowsprit, the horizon was the colour of slate. On the port bow, the Wolf Rock was a smudge of white water crowned with a rusty iron beacon. To starboard, the Longships growled unlit. And far ahead, where the beacons of the Bishop and the Seven Stones now sweep the sky, there was emptiness; a chaotic world, waiting for order.

The young man who would impose order on this world was in the *Lord Wellington*'s saloon, being sick into a bucket. He was dressed in a London tailor's notion of clothes suitable for a *promenade en mer*. He was clean-shaven, brushed and neat. In this year 1834, with William IV on the throne and Byron not ten years dead, the craggier outposts of Britain were liberally sprinkled with delicately nurtured young men in search of powerful sensations. Most of these retreated swiftly, having failed to penetrate the layer of filth with which the new sensations were liberally smeared. But there was much about this gentleman that spoke of an unwillingness to retreat. He had stayed at Pearce's Union Hotel in Penzance, with the life-mask of Nelson looking down from the gallery. The beauty and nobility of Penzance had been impressed by his youth, his steadiness, and his crispness of address. The general

assumption was that he was some sort of lord. It was a shock to them, and others who met him in later life, to discover that he was no sort of lord; that his name, indeed, was plain Mr Smith, and that he was exceedingly proud of this fact. It was even more of a shock that a young man of such obvious promise seemed to be planning to become landlord of the Isles of Scilly, thirty-odd miles west of Penzance pierhead.

Then as now, Penzance was not exactly central – London was two days away by coach, if the traveller was lucky. But compared to Scilly, Penzance was practically metropolitan. Scilly (said the people of Penzance) was a group of three hundred and sixty five islands, one for each day of the year[1], inhabited by smugglers, pirates and other forms of violent pauper. There were six inhabited islands, only one of which, St Mary's, was worth considering. There were more shipwrecks than trees. The only legitimate trades were pilotage, fishing and agriculture. But there were few pilots, the populace were too lazy to go fishing, and farming tended to produce a few baskets of early potatoes, some mouldy barley, and pigs like

The passage to Scilly from Penzance was a memorable one. Sailings were on Friday mornings. Once he was established on Scilly, Augustus Smith was generally collected from the packet by his own boatmen in St Mary's Sound. On arrival at the Abbey he restored the tissues with large quantities of vermicelli soup.

1. It is a geographical truth that most archipelagoes are said by people who do not know them to contain exactly 365 islands.

Penzance before the railways. The skyline is largely unchanged. The white house in the foreground is Ponsondane, home of a branch of the great Bolitho banking family.

whippets, only slower and fiercer. The inhabitants of St Mary's knew how to take care of themselves after a fashion. The inhabitants of the rest of Scilly, the off-islands (said Penzance) were not far removed from the brute creation, living for much of the year on limpets, which they called sea beef.

That was another very bad thing about Scillonians. They led lives perpetually on the brink of disaster, but often they seemed incapable of taking anything seriously. The only really good thing about the Isles of Scilly, (reckoned Penzance) was that they could not be seen from Penzance, and being out of sight were also out of mind, except on Fridays, when the sailing packet *Lord Wellington* sailed from the town quay, weather permitting (it frequently did not).

Down in the saloon, Mr Smith was seen (in the intervals between retching fits) to be writing in a little black book. As the *Lord Wellington* thumped the head sea round the south of St Mary's and came into St Mary's Sound, her motion eased. Mr Smith came on deck, and stood hunched in his greatcoat, watching the dark loom of the islands: St Agnes to port, bearing the feeble gleam of Scilly's only lighthouse, St Mary's to starboard, the Garrison hill rising to the yellow gutter of candlelight in Star Castle. There was a crowd waiting on St Mary's crumbling dogleg quay. The shore lines went onto the bollards and were hauled in. The passengers struggled ashore.

The smell of old Scilly rose to Mr Smith's nostrils. In the foreground was essence of St Mary's harbour – rotting seaweed and foul drains from the town beach, an effluvium of seldom-washed bodies from the crowd on the quay, and the sour hum percolating from the *Lord Wellington*'s saloon skylight. But behind this stink was a smell of warm rock and heather. And behind that, ozone, cleaned by a four-thousand-mile passage over open ocean. Mr Smith drew a deep breath and stepped onto the quay. He was greeted by an anxious, well-dressed man who introduced himself as W.T. Johns. Mr Smith returned the greeting with civility but without effusion, and suffered his bags to be carried ashore.

Later that night, he walked up the hill to the Garrison, the western hill of St Mary's.

The gun emplacements were half-ruinous. What rebuilding had been done seemed to have had as its object the confinement of several sheep that cropped the fine grass among the guns. A heifer bellowed from her stall, which also did duty as the magazine. Mr Smith walked on to the summit. To the north, Samson, Bryher and Tresco were treeless humps, scattered with a few – a minute few – points of yellow light. To the east, Hugh Town was a thicker cluster of candle-lit windows, Crow Sound and St Martin's looming beyond. To the west, beyond the feeble glow of the St Agnes light, the charts marked rocks, hedge after hedge of them, marching ten miles towards America. Overhead, the stars crusted a sky so clear and dark that they hardly twinkled. Mr Smith was used to the Home Counties. The emptiness of these islands affected him powerfully.

Scilly belonged to the Duchy of Cornwall, which had absent-mindedly slipped the archipelago into its pocket at the Dissolution of the Monasteries. It had leased them in 1571 to the Godolphins, and subsequently to the Godolphin descendant the Duke of Leeds, the son of whose ex-agent had greeted Mr Smith on the quay. In 1829 the Duke had refused to renew the lease, and Scilly had found itself without a Lord Proprietor.

This meant much more than the mere absence of a landlord. From the Lord Proprietor came all authority on Scilly. Without the Lord Proprietor there could be no courts, civil or criminal. The Duchy of Cornwall, which could have stepped in to restore order, did not. The Bishop of Exeter, en route to rectify the chaotic state of Anglicanism in the island, had spent the first half of his passage on the *Lord Wellington* expecting to die, and the second half wishing he could. He had gone home to Exeter resolved thenceforward to blank Scilly from his mind.

In this state of anarchy, the St Mary's shopkeepers were making a tolerable living, thanks to an enlightened policy of nepotism and petty corruption. The off-islanders, however, were in a state of starvation – it was one of the curiosities of Scilly that the sounds separating St Mary from the off-islands were to all intents and purposes wider than the stretch of water separating Hugh Town from Penzance.

On the islands looming darkly around Mr Smith there was a lack of law, religion, education, food and clean water. The population was criminalised, pauperised and oppressed. The land was poor, the seas huge, the weather atrocious. Chaos reigned on every hand. Famine and disease threatened horrors imaginable and unimaginable.

It was exactly the sort of place Mr Smith had been looking for.

ONE

Wild but Useful

THE REAL horror in Mr Smith's life lay just north of London, in the green and over-civilised Hertfordshire countryside. Berkhamstead, once a rural market town, was exactly the right distance from London to form the centre of a cluster of estates owned by minor noblemen and merchants who had made major fortunes.

The Smith family had arrived there by the latter route. In the second half of the seventeenth century, Thomas Smith, a mercer of Nottingham, had noticed that while it was possible to get rich by selling cloth, it was possible to get richer by lending money to his customers and trading in their unpaid bills. Before long, he was a banker – the first outside London. Thomas's son Samuel founded Samuel Smith & Sons, bankers and Turkey merchants, importers of porcelain and carpets and painted wallpapers.

In 1800, the seven sons of Samuel Smith sold the business to Bosanquet's of Lombard Street, turned their backs on commerce, and bought estates. In 1801 James Smith, one of the seven, bought Ashlyns Hall in Hertfordshire – a suitable house for a merchant who knew what he wanted, with every comfort, healthful gravel soil, and plenty of the right sort of neighbours. Frankly, the Smiths by this point had become somewhat smug and sobersided, with more money than was helpful to elasticity of opinion. Among the neighbours were some Dorriens, similarly sobersided ex-bankers, trying to live down an eighteenth century financing privateers to loot Spanish treasure fleets; and more significantly some Pechells. The Pechells were descended from Huguenot aristocrats who had come to England after the Revocation of the Edict of

Ashlyns. The epitome of solid comfort, bought by Augustus Smith's father. Augustus was deeply attached to the garden, planted by his mother. This late nineteenth-century photograph, probably taken when the house was rented to the publishing Longman family, shows a corner of the original plantings.

Nantes in 1685. They were a close family, much given to celebrations, al fresco dinners, the writing of special songs for special occasions, and other immodesties calculated to freeze Smith blood. James Smith had the great good taste to marry Mary Isabella Pechell in 1803, a year after the death of his first wife. And in September 1804, Augustus John Smith was born at the house of a fashionable *accoucheur* in Harley Street.

Having been born in the best and safest circumstances available, Augustus Smith's early upbringing continued in the same vein. He lived at Ashlyns, surrounded by friends and cousins in what amounted to a heavily gilded outer suburb of London. His life was even, luxurious, and by the standards of the early nineteenth century safe as houses – except for two great disasters. First, his elder half-brother James was killed when he fell from his pony in the Ashlyns drive. Then, as he was leaving Harrow, his mother died while on a visit to Paris. The Ashlyns Smiths had been a close, happy family. Losing his brother had been a great disaster to the six-year-old. Losing his mother was an immeasurably more shocking blow. Her Pechell brightness had passed on to him as a capacity for lightheartedness not found in earlier Smiths, and he spoke later of her skill in the choosing and arrangement of plants to make a garden 'with which my boyhood is identified.' Her death tightened his bonds to his siblings and closened his friendships with them.

The young Augustus was a private man, inclined to draw his own conclusions. This meant that what he did often surprised his neighbours. When he left Oxford in 1826, the grandees of the Berkhamstead area expected him to sow a wild oat or two, put his large personal fortune into an estate with a hefty rent-roll, then start looking about him for a well-heeled wife with whom to share a well-padded Smith life. But Augustus found the Smith padding not so much comfortable as suffocating. Furthermore, he had developed an acute sense of the ridiculous, married to a passion for justice, which, as he began to take note of politics, made him very uncomfortable in the Duke of Wellington's Tory England. The cult of aristocracy was a powerful part of Toryism, and some Smiths – the Carringtons, for instance – had discovered noble forbears in the Middle Ages and adopted names and coats of arms to suit. Augustus Smith considered this an absurdity, and was proud to be an ordinary Englishman – though it is fair to say that not many other people regarded him as ordinary at all.

In the England of the 1830s, the poor were entirely disregarded by the rich. It was ordained (thought the Tories) that some people were born fortunate, and many others less so: God made them high or lowly and ordered their estate. The poor were miserably paid and dismissed at will. If their earnings proved insufficient to support life, they were subsidised by a poor rate levied on the wealthier classes and distributed at the discretion of local Poor Law Commissioners. It was a system that penalised the industrious labourer, who was hired at small wages by farmers who relied on the poor rate to supply the shortfall. Drunks and slackers, however, were kept bumping along the potatoes-and-gin line by the Commissioners' handouts. In Berkhamstead, as almost everywhere else in England, the upper middle classes and the aristocracy subscribed unthinkingly to the notion that this was the way things had always been and ever more would be.

Even as a young man, Augustus had very little time for orthodoxies, Tory or otherwise. He liked to work things out from first principles. Watching the high play and crass debaucheries of his Oxford contemporaries, he had begun to evolve a new set of certainties. At some point during his Oxford career, he had fallen under the influence of the Utilitarian sage Jeremy Bentham.

Bentham is best remembered now for his eccentricities. He is famous for bombarding Prince Potemkin with recipes for ideal societies to be formed from reorganized Cossack hordes.

By family tradition, this is either Augustus Smith or his elder half brother James, killed in a riding accident in 1810. The park, in the foothills of the Chilterns, breathes a calm, civilised, Home-Counties air. The house may be an idealised representation of Ashlyns.

Disliking the fuss attendant on funerals, he had himself dried, and can still be seen goggling alarmingly from a glass case in University College, London. But it is helpful in understanding the wellsprings of Augustus's unconventional thought to glance at the profoundly sensible basics of Bentham's moral philosophy.

Useful actions performed by individual humans are actions that cause pleasure, not pain. A large number of actions that are useful – 'have utility', as Bentham put it – will affect the whole of society in a positive way. The usefulness of social policies can be measured by their positive effect on the well-being of the majority of the population. In time, these policies will tend to promote equality of opportunity, if not of achievement. This differs sharply from Tory *laisser-faire*, which makes a few people happy at a cost of the misery of the many, virtually denies that individuals can improve their lot through their own efforts, and pays no heed to the social usefulness of policies and individual acts.

It seemed obvious to Augustus Smith, looking at the Home Counties in the 1820s, that the best way to have a positive effect on the well-being of the population was to raise standards of education. 'When I found youths, the progeny of hereditary paupers, simply through being able to read, write and cipher, readily obtain in London apprenticeships in various trades, I felt the true or at least the main clue was discovered.' Augustus therefore began a campaign to revive the fortunes of Berkhamstead Grammar School, and to establish parish schools.

Berkhamstead Grammar School was an ancient foundation, and none the better for it. It had no pupils. This fact did not prevent the headmaster from drawing his wages. He was understandably suspicious of a change in the status quo. Smith's Parish Schools were to be non-denominational – open to Nonconformists like Methodists and Baptists, and so more attractive to the working classes than institutions run by the frankly Tory Church of England.

Smith's Parish Schools taught the 3 Rs, and useful trades. As soon as the local wealth and nobility, many of them regular diners at Ashlyns, heard of this Godless interference with the indissoluble union of Church and King, they struck back. They opened a string of Church schools, dedicated to the teaching of Scripture Knowledge and not much else, which they supported with valuable grants of money and land. Augustus – now in his mid-twenties – was left to support his own schools from his own means. The Tories sat back, waiting for him to be crushed by this

Augustus Smith a year or two after his 21st birthday. The jaw is already resolute, the eye steady, the gaze Imperial.

burden. They were disappointed. Augustus, demonstrating the energy that would serve him well in later life, rapidly enlisted the aid of the nondenominational British and Foreign Schools Society, which kept his schools open for some forty years, until in 1870 they were taken over under the Elementary Education Act.

The Grammar School campaign was less successful. Then as now, it was hard to break up the cement of mutual backscratching that held together the establishment of an English market town. It reopened, principally to teach Greek and Latin. Augustus was scornful. 'It is more agreeable to [these people] to raise the school to the level of Eton and Harrow than to [be] useful . . . for the sons of tallow-chandlers, tailors, drapers, farmers, publicans and dealers in muffins, coal and coffins.'

Mr Smith had cut his teeth on Berkhamstead battles, but

they were not in the end sufficiently challenging. There was a tameness about Berkhamstead founded in centuries of usage, and a wildness about Augustus that made him long to institute a usage of his own.

In 1831 he heard about the mess Scilly had become, and opened preliminary negotiations with the Duchy of Cornwall. But HM Commissioner of Woods and Forests suddenly (and rather quixotically) laid claim to the islands, and began a squabble with the Duchy. Augustus, not a man who enjoyed taking bureaucratic crossfire, withdrew. In 1833 he was in Ireland, meditating taking a lease on the beautiful (but completely useless) Aran Islands. At Ballynahinch Castle in Connemara he met the novelist Maria Edgeworth, who at first saw only the Smith in him, and put him down as a Home Counties prig. Deeper acquaintance made her warm to him, and she praised his sense and originality of mind – which probably sat well with hers. Her father had been a member of the Birmingham Lunar Society (as had Matthew Bolton, Josiah Wedgwood, and Erasmus Darwin, grandfather of Charles: men at the cutting edge of the Enlightenment, with a powerful scientific and social curiosity). At Edgeworthstown, Maria's home, the domestic cistern was filled by a pump that automatically dispensed one penny per hundred strokes to beggars. This was the kind of neat and useful solution that Augustus greatly enjoyed.

In the end, though, Ireland with its horrible tenancy systems of runrig and conacre was too *laisser-mourir* for Augustus. Rejecting notions of colonization, he returned to Hertfordshire, and continued his educational battles with what looked like singlemindedness. But it was one of his great talents to be singleminded about several different things at the same time.

He was happy in the company of his family, particularly his little sister Paulina, now twelve, to whom in the absence of their mother he had become very close, and whose company encouraged in him the fantastical, unbankerish Pechell vein that delighted in silly riddles. (What did a blind man take at breakfast and recovered his sight? He took a cup and saw-sir!) But there was a sort of restlessness about him, as of a man trying not to get drawn back into a mainstream of grand bourgeois life. Augustus Smith was a Georgian social experimenter in the Lunar Society tradition, fire in his belly and a glint in his eye, a believer in Benjamin Franklin's maxim that 'anger is a sinew of the soul, and he who wants it has a maimed mind.' His mission was not gently to steer

St Agnes – a drawing probably from the 1830s, showing the old lighthouse and the Punchbowl in the centre. St Agnes rock lies under a thin skin of peaty soil, and the ground is thickly strewn with boulders.

institutions, but to tear up the old and install the radical new.

Then in 1834, the Duchy of Cornwall won its lawsuit against the Commissioner of Woods and Forests, and wrote to Augustus informing him that the Isles of Scilly were once again available.

* * *

Life on Scilly had been going steeply downhill since the end of the Napoleonic war, when the islands had been a refuge for shipping on the run from enemy privateers. The Council of Twelve, which drew its authority from the Duke of Leeds, had become a byword for sleepiness, then lost its *raison d'être* when the Duke gave up the lease. Since Scilly was Crown land, nobody could own property. Nobody who did not own property could be a JP, so there was no bench of magistrates, and therefore no law. There were no property taxes, or indeed taxes of any kind; so there was no money for public works, or indeed to escort criminals to Bodmin Assizes, or to pay their keep in Bodmin jail when they were convicted. In the absence of licensing laws any house could sell drink, and an astonishing number did.

Scilly stands behind its rocky fortifications at a crossroads in the sea. In the days of sail, it was a natural place for a ship riding the prevailing westerlies to pick up a pilot who would show her the way to London, Bristol or Liverpool. Pilotage had indeed become the principal industry of the islands. Deep-drafted cutters cruised a hundred miles to the west of the Bishop Rock to put pilots on vessels bound up the English, Bristol or St George's Channels. Closer to the islands, six- or

Bringing in bracken for winter bedding on St Martin's.

A typical pilot boat. The man on the foredeck gives an idea of her enormous draught. The sails are stowed in the industrial rather than the yachting manner – the jib merely dropped on deck, the main still hoisted, but scandalized by dropping the gaff peak and hauling in the tricing line.

seven-oared gigs raced to put inshore or branch pilots onto vessels bound for Scilly itself. Then in 1811 Trinity House, the ancient (and unaccountable) body responsible for lights and pilotage round Britain's coasts, had taken it upon itself to limit the number of licensed pilots to 32, 24 of whom – a disproportionate number – belonged to St Mary's. The Trinity House agent was a St Mary's man, and tended to appoint his friends and relations, many of whom 'were not accustomed to the sea.' Smuggling, usually on a small scale and a by-product of piloting, had been destroyed by harsh new Preventive laws, under which a pilot boat could be seized if so much as a pound of undutied sugar was discovered on board.

Farming was another problem area. Agriculture – practised on the off-islands mostly at subsistence level – was notionally important on Scilly. But islanders enjoyed family life. Over the years, parents had divided their holdings between their children, who had done the same with their own children. The rent rolls were now hopelessly confused, subletting was rife, and most of the individual holdings were too small to support their occupiers. In the early 1830s on St Agnes, an island with a total farmable area of perhaps half a square mile, there were 433 parcels of land.

In 1818, while St Mary's exported potatoes to the mainland, there was famine in the off-islands. The vast sum of £10,000 was raised for relief. A small part of this was used to set up a pilchard fishery, with fish-processing cellars on Tresco, nets and boats. These fell into disuse, were washed away, and rotted. The balance of the money, administered by General Smyth of the St Mary's Garrison, mysteriously disappeared.

When the Rev. Woodley of the SPCK mission to the islands attempted an informal audit of a further £100 and 100 quarters of barley, intended for the relief of the off-islanders but distributed among the General's cronies, the General dismissed him with 'oaths and insults.'

It was this same General Smyth, a member of what passed for a ruling clique on St Mary's, who said in 1831 – when Scilly was at its lowest ebb since the 1818 famine – that the islands were 'becoming places of greater consequence year by year.' It might just have been possible to feel this optimism on St Mary's during strong easterly breezes, with the harbour full of bottled-up ships waiting for the wind to turn westerly and blow them up-Channel. Then 'butchers and bakers increased their returns, and the farmers had a better market for their produce.' Otherwise, one can only assume that the General, not a person of powerful imagination, was pointing out that he personally had never had it so good.

On the termination of the Leeds tenancy, the Duchy of Cornwall sent the surveyors George and Edward Driver to the islands to compile a report on the islands' potential. The Drivers were a highly reputable firm, but their report shows a becoming consciousness of who they were working for. They admitted that things at Scilly were perhaps not as they should have been, particularly as regarded the leases, which were in a state of confusion. They were baffled by the Scillonian acre, which was either bigger or smaller than the statute acre, depending on who they were talking to, and was in either case calculated by 'using a piece of rope in a particular way.' They were horrified by the fact that the Duke of Leeds' agent had

An idyllic washday at Porth Hellick on St Mary's in the pre-Smith era. The sea is calm, the women carrying baskets of laundry to dry on the gorse bushes inland of the cottage while the men build haycocks. The large, curved timbers in the foreground, and the jagged rocks in the background, give a hint that life is not always this peaceful.

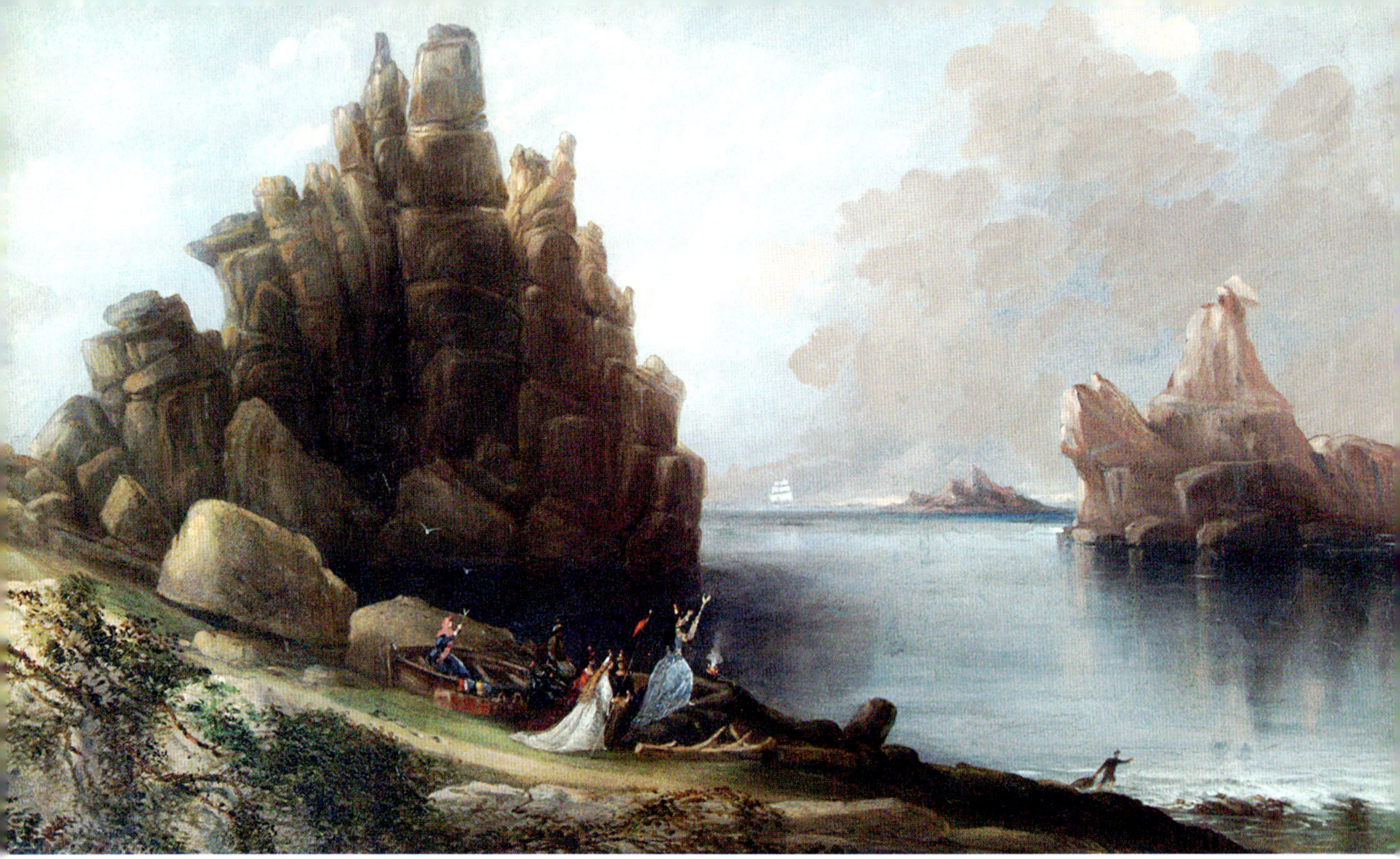

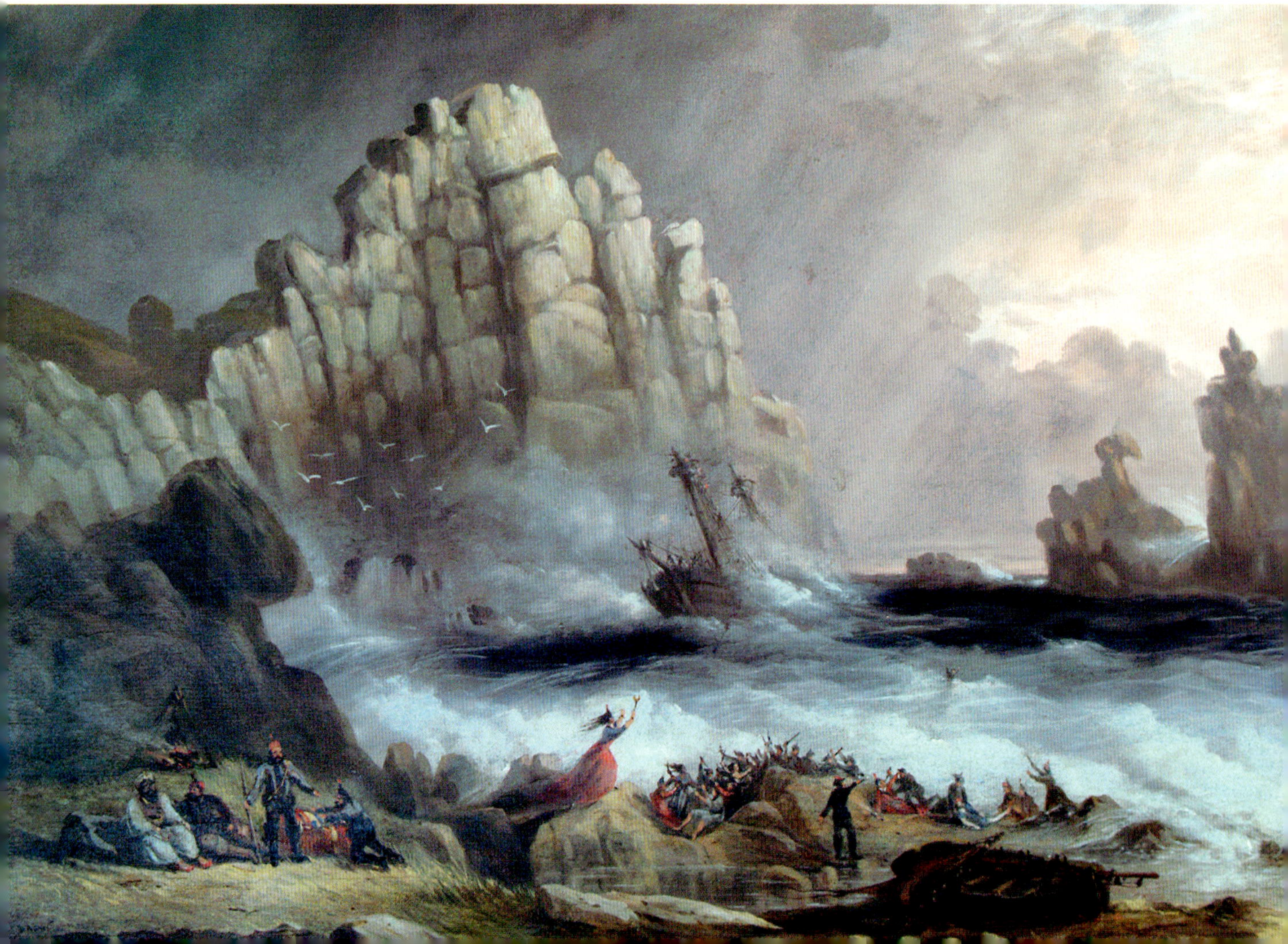

allowed £4,000 of rent arrears to accumulate and seemed to have no idea where many of the farms were. But despite all this (they concluded, allowing their eyes to sweep lovingly over limitless vistas of pauperism, anarchy and petty corruption) there were splendid possibilities. It was just a matter of getting the right – by which they meant higher – rents for the farms.

A less acute man than Augustus Smith would have noticed that the Drivers were trying to sell a basket case by describing the exquisite construction of the basket. A less acute man than Smith would have turned his back on the whole shambles and bucketed his way back to the mainland on the first available boat. But Scilly fitted Smith's nature very well. It was wild and beautiful, and he had a profound enthusiasm for wildness and beauty. By virtue of its position it was self-contained, so the consequences of his actions would begin and end inside the archipelago. And at that moment it was a blank slate, without taxes, regulation or even the means of subsistence. Jeremy Bentham once remarked that the first calling of man is jurisprudence. Scilly in 1834 was a jurisprudentialist's paradise.

Augustus walked down from the Garrison and was conducted round the islands. That autumn he signed a lease and became Lord Proprietor of the Isles of Scilly.

ABOVE Old Grimsby, Tresco, in the early years of the Smith prosperity. The grey house on the extreme left stands on the site now occupied by the Island Hotel. The cottages are thatched with heather anchored by nets of rope weighted with stones. The roads are metalled with ram, a form of decomposed granite. Curiously, the sun appears to be setting in the north.

OPPOSITE PAGE TOP St Warna in her cove on St Agnes. The sea is calm, the weather benign, the breeze fair for the Channel. St Warna, accompanied by a motley crew (which seems to include several Turks), is about to do her duty by the impoverished inhabitants, who traditionally summoned her by throwing bent pins into her well. Spotting a ship in the offing, she raises her wand . . .

OPPOSITE PAGE BELOW . . . with results helpful to the inhabitants, but not to the ship. Augustus Smith, who owned these paintings, was unenthusiastic about superstition, but a romantic at heart.

23

TWO

Mr Smith Grasps the Nettle

T HE DUCHY of Cornwall sold Augustus Smith a lease on the Isles of Scilly for 99 years or three lives from November 20, 1834. In return, Augustus Smith paid the Duchy a fine of £20,000 and a rent of £40 a year. He also agreed to spend £5,000 on the new church and the new pier at St Mary's, and agreed to be responsible for choosing and employing clergy and teachers for the islands. The rent seems small, the fine large. This is because fines payable at the beginning of leases were at that time counted by lessors not as capital sums, but as income. Augustus's money was therefore available for immediate spending.

Many issues, notably the ownership of wreck washed ashore on the islands, were not specifically covered in the lease. Augustus, a loyal and trusting subject of William IV and full of enthusiasm that this great project was now his, seems for once in his life to have skated over the detail. He had taken the Drivers' prospectus with a large pinch of salt. But he had not expected the Duchy, which he considered to represent the King he respected, almost immediately to start going back on its promises. It was a rude disillusionment, and one that would deepen as the years passed.

Throughout 1834, rumours had been flying. Island soothsayers had naturally seen their new landlord coming. He was the son of a rich India merchant and a beautiful native girl, they maintained, losing their natural caginess in their excitement. He had lent the King money when the King had

A rare glimpse of pre-Smith St Mary's, from the Garrison. A sketch from the 1830s – possibly by Augustus Smith himself – showing the old quay with its dogleg end. With one ship alongside and another on the beach, the harbour is to all intents and purposes full.

been the seagoing Duke of Clarence, and the King had sold him the islands cheap. Nonsense, declared other, rival mystics. Augustus had been hurt by love, and had come to drown his grief by wild acts of charity towards the unfortunate Scillonians.

Augustus Smith treated rumours as he treated ghosts and lawyers; he paid them absolutely no attention. Looking neither right nor left, he marched up to his difficulties and began to grapple with them. In March 1835, he and five others took their Oaths as Magistrates for the islands. Augustus was chairman. Among the others were General Smyth, the suspected embezzler, Captain Veitch, RN retired, and Mr John Hall, Collector of Customs. No clergymen were to be asked onto the bench, because of their propensity for causing trouble. Augustus had already engaged W.T. Johns, son of the John Johns who had been the Duke of Leeds' agent and a key member of the St Mary's establishment, as his agent. Johns, an experienced Scillonian, eagerly agreed to be his spokesman as well as his man of business. He vowed not to gossip (except in cases where it would be useful). 'I assure you that I shall consider all your communications private and confidential,' he wrote, adding that the roof of the Chaplain's house was unsafe. By his next letter, the Chaplain's roof had actually fallen in.

Augustus Smith was now committed to a lifetime's work in Scilly. The idea seemed for a short, nervous period to afflict him with a mixture of timidity and pride, which manifested

25

Gigs and a crowd at Porthcressa, St Mary's. In the background on the right is the Hugh House, principal ornament of Hugh Town, briefly inhabited by Augustus Smith after his arrival in the islands. It now houses the Scilly offices of the Duchy of Cornwall.

itself as arrogance. He sent Johns detailed specifications for major alterations to the Johns residence required before he would deign to stay there. And he arranged for the restoration of the Hugh House, a grim lump of a building that scowls over Hugh Town from the eastern flanks of Garrison Hill. Johns sent him dismal letters about the state of the harbour and the potato market. He sent lists of troublesome tenants. Shortly after his swearing-in as a magistrate, Augustus Smith was behind his desk in Johns' rebuilt rooms, going through Scilly like a hot knife through butter, swiftly earning the title, half-ironic, half-respectful, of Emperor.

He had boiled his plans for Scilly down to four main points. First, every child in the islands was going to get an education. Second, he planned to consolidate the tenant farms into holdings of economic size. Third, he planned to eradicate smuggling by providing well-paid employment for all, based on the provision and use of a new infrastructure on the islands. And fourth, he planned to give his tenants security of tenure, and thus the incentive to improve their property.

Some called this Benthamism, others common sense. Whatever it was called, it was extremely unpopular. The consolidation of holdings meant many evictions, which in turn would lead to the breakdown of the informal Scillonian system of welfare in which cousins looked after cousins (which all too often amounted to little more than a sharing of limpets). Smuggling was the Scillonian national sport, which in its mixture of danger and exhilaration occupied roughly the same

niche as foxhunting on the mainland. As for going to school, there were already SPCK mission schools on the islands (though their curriculum was very limited, consisting largely of Scripture knowledge). Old Scilly muttered and grumbled. Someone said, 'If your honour would only get rid of the Preventive Service, we would do very well.' Smith laughed at this. He would not have been the only one. One of the things he shared with the Scillonians was a highly-developed sense of irony.

Meanwhile, he was looking for a site for his house. The inhabitants of St Mary's are to this day surprised that he did not choose their island. They point to Holy Vale, a well-watered valley that supported Scilly's only trees, as a perfect spot for a gentleman's residence. But Holy Vale was already the home of the prominent Mumford family, and the views, while southerly, are of a bay crossed by a blue horizon. It is the kind of view you can find elsewhere in the West Country. Furthermore, the bourgeoisie of St Mary's was capable, on a bad day, of making the island feel like a sort of miniature Berkhamstead.

Tresco, second biggest of the islands, had freshwater ponds, the whitest beaches in the world, a certain amount of fertile soil, and two harbours. The site Augustus finally chose, by a ruined abbey on a rocky ridge overlooking the southern end of the island, is more or less in the middle of Scilly. Before Tresco's trees grew to their present height, all the islands of Scilly would have been visible from the summit of the ridge. It is perhaps unwise to labour Smith's Benthamite tendencies too

Houses at Old Grimsby. The barrel contains water. Fish – probably ling, a Scillonian and Cornish staple – and washing are drying in the sun.

Mary Nance of Tresco outside the front door of her cottage. Her black shawl is typical of the islands in the mid-19th century, as is the construction of her front porch – massive boulders, exquisitely laid with one flat face, and a curious cement roof.

Pendarves house in the late 18th century. It was owned by friends of Augustus Smith, but he did not approve of what he called its 'workhouse look'.

far; but the site of Tresco Abbey does have certain points of resemblance to Bentham's Panopticon, the model prison or factory in which the inmates are at all times visible to the warden without being visible to each other.

The Abbey site is the best in the islands. Augustus had great faith in the capacity of monks to make themselves comfortable, and he gave them the credit; but as usual, he had looked long and chosen once. As ever, his self-interest had an enlightened quality. The choice of Tresco as a dwelling was a vote of confidence in the starving off-islands, and one in the eye for smug St Mary's. The inhabitants of Tresco and next-door Bryher, used to doing pretty much as they wished, may not at first have found Augustus Smith's presence in their midst very relaxing. But they soon got used to the idea; he made sure of that.

The Abbey arose from Augustus's conversations with friends and masons. In its original form his new house was a simple building, with a big drawing room, two gables, and the smallest bedrooms his guests had ever seen – 'cabins', he called them. An early drawing of the building arising from the fumes of conversation, stark on its treeless bluff, hints at a deeper logic to the place. Smith had been a Mason since he had been of age. He wrote disparagingly of the plainness of Cornish houses. The new house at Tresco was built of Cyclopean lumps of granite, with one flat face, otherwise shaped as they had been split out of the quarry by the expansion of wooden wedges soaked in water. His trademark corbels lighten the junction of the wall and roof, and the glass of the drawing room windows is set directly into the rebates

The first sketch of Tresco Abbey. No more than a large cottage at this early stage, it seems to be being talked into existence by the grotesque heads on either side.

of chamfered mullions of granite. The timbers were of wreckwood. It was a house in which many people could live without treading on each other's toes – usefully, in a place where thanks to the packet boat schedules the minimum stay would be a week[2].

* * *

Tacked on the eastern end was a small private suite of rooms for the Proprietor's use, to which he could come and go unobserved by others in the house. This was convenient for a hard-working man with a houseful of guests. It also provided access for people he did not wish his guests to meet.

As the walls rose course by course from the bare hillside, there were those who thought Mr Smith engaged in a folly. What they did not yet realise was that he brought to his whimsies and amusements the same energy and consistency as to his reform of leases or his improvement of the Berkhamstead schools.

They very soon learned.

Meanwhile, jurisprudence occupied the public Smith. After complaints of 'tippling, dancing, card-playing, etc etc,' he decreed via the newly-appointed magistrates that pubs were to close at eleven p.m. and during church services. This was a liberal enough regime, but then Augustus was no enemy of gaiety and detested fanatics, including teetotallers. He continued to make policy, poring with engineers and architects over the plans for the remarkable works to extend St Mary's quay and build the Church.

The Bench of Magistrates, meanwhile, took on the characteristics of a soap opera. General Smyth, overruled in acts of petty spite against Clement Mumford, grew increasingly sulky – a sulkiness perhaps aggravated by the fact that since Mr Smith's arrival, he was no longer Scilly's First Citizen. Peter Pender, mate of the *Navarino*, was fined 15/6d for having indecently exposed his person at the house of Anne Banfield on Tresco Green. Mr Hall, Inspector of Customs, declared himself unable to move a full and leaking privy without orders from the mainland. Subletting tenants were warned that they would be evicted in October.

Augustus went to the mainland for the summer. When he returned in the autumn, it was with a sense of growing

---

2. This policy found its fullest expression in Tregarthen's Hotel, St Mary's. Captain Tregarthen, owner of the hotel, was also the captain of the packet. There were persistent rumours that when hotel business was slow, packet sailings were mysteriously delayed.

Paulina, younger sister and dearest friend of Augustus, who was to her always the Lord Proprietor of the Rocks of Scilly.

affection and involvement. He was getting to know people. But most of his delight in life came from the fact that he had real company in his house for the first time. He had brought his favourite sister Paulina down to stay – now fifteen years old, dark and pretty. She was an amusing girl, and her vein of fantasy was as good as a tonic to Augustus, tired by the effort of keeping a straight face in the muddle and farce of Scilly under reform. For Paulina's part, she loved dear Augustus with a deep and uncritical admiration. In the absence of their dead mother, each was the other's closest companion in life.

One autumn evening, Augustus took Paulina to the launch of a ship in St Mary's harbour – a great island jollification, with lashings of tea and a special cake. The night turned dank and chilly. Paulina caught cold. The cold settled on her lungs. She took to her bed in the House on the Bank, now known as the Atlantic Hotel – in those days a miserably damp place, where the wallpaper peeled off the walls in three days unless fires were kept constantly lit. The doctor was called, to no avail. On October 30th, she died.

It was a terrible blow, and it marks an epoch in Augustus Smith's relationship with Scilly. He departed the islands, escorting poor Paulina's body up country for burial in the family vault at Berkhamstead. He did not come back for the best part of a year. His communications with the agent Johns took on a theoretical remoteness. He suggested a stocking-knitting industry on Bryher (where the women hated doing it, and expressed their dislike by overcharging shockingly) and the use of communal ovens to bake the island bread (the women liked to use their own ovens). Johns bent practically double in his attempts at tactful demurral. A note of real emergency enters his letters. Tenants who had never heard of Jeremy Bentham were resisting eviction. The new mill, ordered by Augustus for the communal grinding of Tresco's barley, was the wrong engine driving the wrong stones in the wrong place (this was not the kind of thing he enjoyed being told). The Brianites, Bible Christians, were hijacking coffins, over which their female preacher then raved weirdly[3].

Augustus Smith's first ecclesiastical hiring, a Mr Willcocks, was spotted by a rival parson ferreting in the country when he should have been conducting a funeral, in consequence of which the Brianites were able to take possession of the coffin. The new farm boundaries had led to a general sense of

[3]. The preacher, one Ann Guest, was paid wages resulting from the sale of a fat pig, which was swum from St Martin's to St Mary's for the purpose.

claustrophobia. On May Eve hooligans smashed windows at the Abbey, now nearly built, and the old habit of turf cutting for fuel – proscribed by Mr Smith in his new leases on pain of eviction – had returned. There is a strong sense in Johns' letters at this point that he was covering up for his fellow Scillonians. And Richard Taylor the shoemaker was for the third time in a year found zigzagging down the Bank, full of drink and swearing at all and sundry.

On the credit side of the account, the reforms were beginning to bite, the Abbey roof was being leaded, and the first stone of the new St Mary's quay, one of the works stipulated in the lease and a feat of logistics without parallel in the history of the islands, had been laid. Poverty was on the run, and the first glow of a new age of prosperity was spreading on the horizon.

* * *

It is hard to avoid the conclusion that at this time Augustus could not think about Scilly – or anyway St Mary's – without thinking about Paulina's death, and more than likely blaming himself for it. But grief could not divert him for ever. By October 1836 he was back in the islands, running an inquest on William Mortimer of St Mary's (drowned while drunk). Augustus Smith had kept up the pressure on the projects, and

Scilly was always ready for a party. This is Nickla Thies, a harvest supper traditionally attended by eating, dancing and general conviviality in the 'House of the Mow'. Other festivals included St Blaze, when crossed candles were held to children's throats as protection against soreness; and May Eve, when effigies were burned and pranks frequently crossed the line into loutishness. Mr Smith was tolerant of folklore, but not of vandalism.

31

The first phase of Tresco Abbey was finished in 1836. Here the ruined Abbey Arch can be seen by the half-built garden wall, next to the last surviving cottage of several in the notoriously unhealthy group round the Abbey Well, now the Pump Garden. At this point there were no trees on the island, except those that Augustus Smith was planting in the shelter of gorse bushes, whose seed he carried in his pocket at all times.

Johns had kept up the momentum. The Abbey was nearly up, the quay in train, St Mary's church (not one of Augustus' favourite projects) rising. It is hard enough to keep the Scillonian world built and maintained in an age of computers and diesel ships and helicopters. Augustus and his men, building by rule of thumb in an age of sailing ships and carthorses, performed feats of construction that would make modern architects and engineers blench. Augustus poured money into the islands, and the St Mary's bourgeoisie began to complain about the total lack of day labourers and jobbing gardeners. Robert Maybee, rather flatteringly described as the Scillonian Poet, contemplated this beehive-like activity with great satisfaction. 'There were not half enough men on the island to do the work,' he said. 'It was said at that time the island was the richest place in the world for the number of people on it.' Inaccurately, without a doubt; but his remarks indicate the roots of the awe Augustus Smith inspired in Scillonians, who less than ten years earlier had been in the grip of famine.

Among the awestruck were not only spectators like Maybee, but the foreman on the pier and the new church, and the masons working on the Abbey and the gardens. Augustus had an insatiable appetite for work, and a truly horrifying grasp of detail. Furthermore he had a habit of turning up where he was least expected, asking awkward questions and pointing out stones improperly laid. This did not add to his popularity. Tresco Abbey masons walked off the job, leaving only drunks to be hired. The drunks reformed, and did the work.

The Lord Proprietor may not have been popular, but he

Blasting rocks between Tresco and Samson. Augustus Smith's improvements were comprehensive and unceasing.

swiftly developed a sort of nimbus of omniscience. Projects began to come in on time and under budget, which was a brand new experience on Scilly, where the Gulf Stream can have a relaxing effect on moral fibre and shovels have long handles, so their use does not hurt the back[4]. Augustus's energy blew all this away.

This is not to say that he was infallible. He was capable of frightful rages – 'terrible as an army with banners.' This could lead him to Draconian acts, born of frustration. His people evicted a certain Mr Bickford from his house by the usual method of unroofing it. Bickford erected a tent of sails and spars alongside the ruins, and moved in. Mr Smith, Chairman of the Bench, sent him to Bodmin jail for vagrancy. Like many incidents of Augustus Smith's early incumbency, this is cloaked in rumour, and its truth is hard to establish. The same is true of the rumour popular in modern Nonconformist circles that their new landlord was given to bricking up Dissenting chapels in the islands. Close inspection reveals that as landlord he had the right to do this – a right that he only exercised, however, when the use of the chapels as schools interfered with his plans for non-sectarian education in the islands.

A period of prosperity unparalleled in history now began. Even the Duchy of Cornwall was behaving remarkably well, supporting Augustus against the Customs in a dispute over ownership of a barrel of wine found floating. A cloud, small but dark, had however appeared on the horizon. Sir George

---

4. A Cornish academic was asked at a symposium whether there was a Gulf Stream equivalent for the Spanish 'mañana'. He replied that he knew no word expressing that degree of urgency.

St Mary's from Carn Morval. The new church is plainly visible to the left of the picture. The Hugh House stands in splendid isolation above the town, and the new quay is just visible end-on. The harbour is thronged with shipping. On the southern horizon is one of the new-fangled steam vessels, outward bound.

Harrison, secretary to the Duchy, had always been well-disposed towards Augustus, perhaps under the prompting of the King himself. But in June 1837 William IV died, and the young Victoria took the throne. Augustus Smith was a straight-talking Georgian, with the Georgian love for experiment, the Georgian lack of prudishness, and the Georgian love of a bright, abusive phrase. Victoria brought to the throne a mimsy distaste for plain speech, an erotophobic prudery and a court of what Augustus described as 'dirty little German potentates', one of whom she eventually married. Augustus had little time for prudery, less for courts, and even less for Germans. The auguries were less than promising.

Meanwhile, the transformation continued in things large and small. Tresco hens were persuaded to sit on partridge eggs (to the delight of the local rats). Grass was being sown on nearby St Helen's and Ganilly, prospective pastures for mouton *pré salé* (the venture failed. White rabbits were installed on St Helen's, and Ganilly became a penal colony for

34

Shipbuilding on the Town Beach at St Mary's. St Mary's shipbuilding began in the 1830s and prospered amazingly in the 1840s and 1850s. Here, the stem and keelson of a new ship are set up on the beach awaiting planks and frames.

The North Terrace at Tresco Abbey, looking down the Pool to the buildings of the farm and the chimney of the notorious mill. A generation later, Augustus Smith's great-nieces were still complaining about the chunks of granite millstone to be found in Tresco bread.

A shoot in the 1840s. Note the sedentary attitude of the guns, the usual crowd of gulls, and the extreme unconcern of the local puffins.

rogue mules). The Tresco mill produced small amounts of bad flour, and the miller was dismissed for drunkenness. Mr Johns had gently to point out that a puffin shoot in September would find no puffins, which had gone to sea by the middle of August. During the Lord Proprietor's absence on the mainland, Johns wrote weekly letters that amounted to lessons on what would and would not work in Scillonian agriculture. These lessons also served to give the agent an ascendancy over his employer that he was unlikely to have enjoyed at the times his employer was on the ground.

There was one step back to every two steps forward, of course. The St Mary's quay was going well. But the Tresco mill was hopeless, grinding little barley and nearly amputating the miller's hand. The ploughing of Tean had gone badly, the ploughmen being otherwise engaged piloting ships up-Channel. T.L. Hall had been accused by two milkmaids of doing something absolutely disgusting to a cow[5].

The population of Samson, suffering from bad wells and wrecked boats, was resisting eviction for its own good. Mr Davies, the St Agnes schoolmaster, a known associate of Brianites, painted the names on the Abbey bedroom doors. General Smyth having left St Mary's, the Master Gunner appointed himself Commandant of the Garrison and ran a small but thriving farm in what had previously been the gun emplacements, ignoring the fact that they belonged to Mr Smith. The Abbey woodwork was being stained a dreadful

5. Mr Hall, a magistrate, acted as prosecutor and defendant in his own case, and acquitted himself without a stain on his character.

> IN THE
> YEAR OF OUR LORD
> 1837
> THIS CHURCH WAS ERECTED
> BY THE MUNIFICENCE OF
> HIS MAJESTY KING WILLIAM IV
> THE SAME WAS COMPLETED AT THE EXPENCE OF
> AUGUSTUS SMITH ESQUIRE

Plaque in St Mary's Church, placed at the west end at Mr Smith's behest. Any trace of bitterness in the second sentence is thought not to be accidental.

reddish brown, the stain removed with boiling water, new, better stain going on, furniture arriving in dribs and drabs from shops on the mainland and the Ashlyns attics. St Mary's new church was finished, its new windows in and leaking dreadfully. The new St Mary's quay had finished settling at its seaward end, and was, amazingly, ready for use.

After 1838, Augustus never spent less than eight months of the year in the islands. He would take one island in hand every year, rebuilding the quay, repairing the church and the housing stock, sitting in the back of the schoolroom to check the quality of the teaching, frowning his way through sermons. This added to his reputation for authoritarianism. Closer examination shows that this arbitrary behaviour was not mere bullying. Augustus was using himself as a one-man focus group to check the public services which would improve the lives and prospects of his tenants.

Revolutionaries have always found it easy to overturn the status quo and impose new rules on a populace. The difficult

St Mary's, looking northwest. The church stands proudly on one side of the harbour, Hugh Town is in excellent repair, and the ships lie alongside Augustus Smith's remarkable new quay.

part comes with the continued application of these rules – and not necessarily from any failing in the rules themselves, or the people expected to live by them. Augustus Smith's rules for Scilly were just, if Draconian. The problems would come when they ran up against outside bodies with rules of their own – particularly if those bodies were governed by rules that Augustus thought were susceptible of improvement.

Other bodies started to cause trouble almost immediately. His new church was appropriated by the Bishop of Exeter soon after it was finished – an annexation greeted by Augustus with a sort of fatalism. 'Lawyers can claim property as Doctors our bodies and Priests our souls – the more any poor wretched mortal can learn to take care of his own property, body and soul, the better, whatever it may be for the three parasitic professions.'

There was more fuss about the new quay, on which he had spent over £4,000 of his own money. He had personally supervised its completion after his contractor, foiled in attempts to pad his bills, had left in disgust. Now he wanted to recoup some of his outlay by charging quay dues. Johns the agent ran into big problems trying to get hard-bitten merchant captains to see the logic of this. The captain of the schooner *Venus* stood in Blewett's Hotel swearing ruin and damnation and refusing to pay a brass farthing till he saw an Act of Parliament, which did not at that point exist. More significantly, the St Mary's Shipping Company, the quay's principal user, attempted to negotiate. Augustus had set dues at 1d a ton. The Shipping Company offered 1/2d a ton, and waited for Gulf Stream mudge and fudge to do the rest. To their horror, Augustus would not give an inch. Two years of muttering from the shareholders (who included Johns the agent) had no effect. The Shipping Company finally agreed to pay up. It had been demonstrated once and for all that there was no point in arguing with Mr Smith.

It was one thing to impose his will on a company run by the worthies and merchants of St Mary's. But there was stiffer opposition waiting.

As usual, Mr Smith went for it bald-headed.

THREE

The Fortunate Isles

SOON AFTER the accession of Queen Victoria, the Duchy of Cornwall fell victim to an attack of amnesia. The money paid by Augustus Smith as a fine at the beginning of his lease had been spent. The Duchy saw a bright and charismatic young man enjoying the benefits of a splendid archipelago. They also saw that all they were getting out of it were a measly forty pounds a year. This was galling. The Duchy, an apparatus of bureaucrats and courtiers, did not take kindly to being galled. The attack of amnesia allowed them to ignore the fact that the splendours of Scilly were entirely of Augustus's making. They persuaded themselves (against the evidence) that Augustus was being grabby, and decided that they would start to grab something back.

It began with a minor, if irritating, incident. The Duchy increased the stipend of the Chaplain of the Isles by £50 a year, and informed Mr Smith that he was to pay this. Augustus refused, upon which the Duchy's lawyers tried to draw him into a squabble about tithes, a subject of numbing technicality that Augustus mastered thoroughly enough to win the argument. The bureaucrats, frustrated, then made the argument more general. The Duchy arrogated to itself all rights not specifically granted in the lease, offering nothing in return. The exercise of power without responsibility is the mark of the despot. As a Benthamite, Augustus was opposed to despots. As an (on the whole) fair-minded and large-hearted human being, he was infuriated by the slippery manoeuvres of

St Mary's Town Beach from the Garrison, showing the west end of the church, many watertight roofs, and ships in various states of build.

courtiers and the self-serving prevarications of bureaucrats. From now on, these struggles on behalf of Scilly against the Duchy became part of the background of his life.

No matter how mischievous the Duchy, the foreground was bright enough to be a distraction. The prosperity of St Mary's was firmly established. The pilots and shipwrights were heavily employed, and farms here and on the off-islands were doing good business with the victualling. There were four shipyards producing newbuilds. 66 different trades were being practised in the islands, labourers could not be got for love nor money, and wages were sky-high.

One sign of success was that in 1840 the SPCK – which had arrived in the early eighteenth century as a missionary organization in a wild outpost of Britain – withdrew from the islands on the grounds that they were no longer sufficiently wild to merit its attention. Augustus took over responsibility for education. There is no actual evidence for the claim that the Proprietor charged attenders 1d a week and non-attenders 2d. But the principle certainly existed. Anyway, the intelligent Scillonians had noticed that education was a good way of getting ahead in life, and flocked to school – adults as well as children.

The syllabus was similar to the one honed in the Berkhamstead schools. It was strictly non-denominational – each pupil was expected to attend the Sunday school of the church of which he or she was a member. All the pupils studied arithmetic, English and a foreign language. In addition boys studied navigation and manual skills like carpentry, and girls needlework and crafts. Augustus was always pleased to mention that of his pupils who went to sea, none sailed before the mast, and many in the captain's cabin. It is worth pointing out that all this happened forty years before education of any kind became compulsory on the mainland.

St Agnes. Augustus Smith was responsible for the repair and maintenance of the church, as of all the other churches in the islands.

Pupils stand very still for the photographer outside the school on St Mary's. A good practical designer of buildings, Augustus Smith had a penchant for the massive – seen here most clearly in the windows, where sheets of glass are puttied directly into rebates cut into stout granite lintels, sills and mullions.

ABOVE Mr Smith's earliest ventures in gardening were in the area around the Abbey Arch. Here it is in the mid-nineteenth century, flanked by two of the agaves of which he was extremely proud. Mr Smith himself can be seen in a blue coat, talking to a gardener. Beyond him his cattle graze on the pasture that did double duty as the island's cricket pitch, and now serves as the heliport.

OPPOSITE PAGE The Abbey Arch, 2004.

There was naturally a more relaxed side to life. Tresco Abbey was one of Britain's newest and most original country houses, with a uniquely hospitable owner. Its remoteness meant that visits were of long duration. In the house, the love of the brilliant and surprising that had brought Augustus Smith to Scilly reached its full expression.

The garden was developing, too. Smiths had always been enthusiastic proprietors of gardens – Augustus Smith's uncle Samuel had been the first employer of Joseph Paxton, later the Duke of Devonshire's amanuensis and designer of the Crystal Palace. Augustus's more scientific friends, like his mentor and fellow mason Sir Charles Lemon of Carclew, near Truro, had already noted the ease with which tender plants could be grown in Cornwall. If Robert Were Fox could grow 200 kinds of citrus fruit in his garden at Rose Hill in Falmouth, it seemed obvious that Tresco, surrounded on all sides by water that

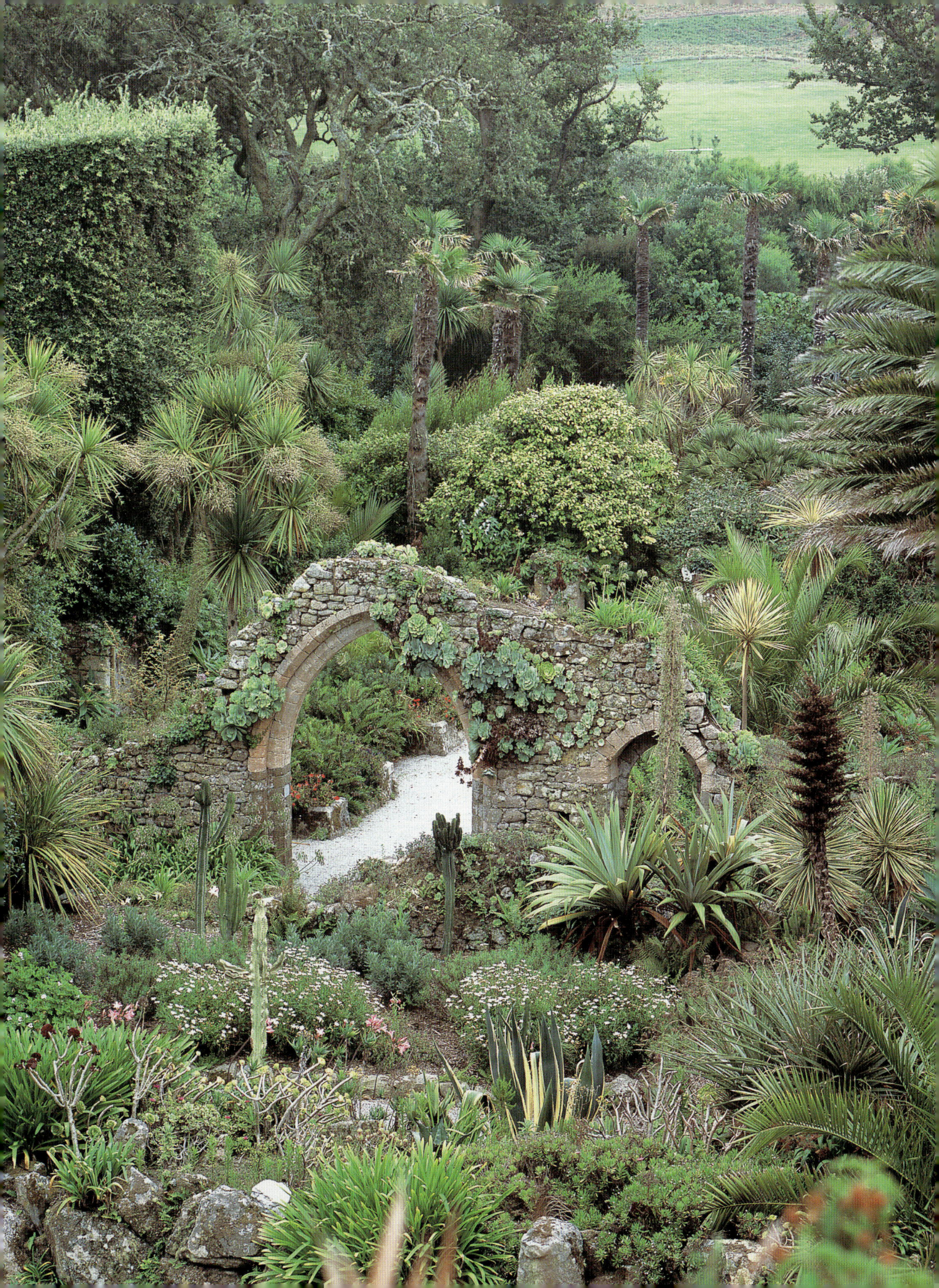

never dropped below 50°, could do as well if not better. But Robert Were Fox was a scientist and a Quaker, who liked the combination of beauty with utility displayed in (for instance) the grapefruit. Mr Smith was famously Mr Smith – not a Quaker, but a free-thinking radical with a whim of iron.

Having established his vegetable garden and exhausted various rose bushes by depriving them of a dormant season – almost entirely absent at Tresco – he looked about him for something interesting to grow. He found it in *Agave Americana ferox*, a conservatory plant on the mainland, which when released from captivity onto the Abbey Hill thrived amazingly[6].

The rocky outcrop on which his new house stood became home to many varieties of South African mesembryanthemum, which he called his 'mesmerisms'. He wrote to Sir William Hooker of Kew in uncharacteristically oily vein, dropping the names of Cornish notables left and right, and soliciting cuttings of hard-to-get varieties. In the letters to Kew there is a new Mr Smith – the collector, single-minded in his desire to get a complete set.

The cultivation of tender plants outdoors became one of the strongest mutual interests of Augustus and his Cornish acquaintance. With some, like John Enys of Enys and Sir Charles Lemon, he spoke of botanical matters[7]. With others, like William Hearle Rodd, natural philosopher and birdwatcher, he discussed the golden oriole and the three types of British shrikes that took up residence in the garden. And with others, improving landlords like Edward Wynne Pendarves and his wife Tryphena, builders of the model village

Not as rare as shrikes and orioles, but distilled essence of Scilly: oyster-catchers, painted by Lady Sophia Tower in the margin of a book.

6. For reasons now lost, since the days of Augustus Smith Agaves have been known on Scilly as Aloes.

7. Lemon seems to have started the careers of the amazing Lobb brothers of Devoran, plant hunters who made Veitch's nursery the staple of British horticulture.

at Treslothan, he discussed the garden as part of an ideal estate regulated along modern lines – a social as well as a scientific asset, to be recorded and appreciated both at once. None of these people had Augustus's exact combination of poetry and practicality. But all of them were his close and trusted friends, anvils on which he hammered out his ideas.

During the 1840s there were other friends who did not form part of the merry throng in the Abbey. In particular there was Mary Pender, who used to visit the suite at the eastern end of the house via a path cut discreetly through the rockery. Two children, Georgiana and Laurence, sprang from this relationship. They and their mother moved to London, where Augustus supported them in great comfort. He seems to have felt no guilt about this arrangement, or another that followed it. There was even a certain propriety in it. To the Georgian mind, it was marriage out of one's class that was improper. Sexual abstinence was unhealthy, and a self-imposed lack of loving companionship perverse. The Victorian mind saw things differently. Mary Anne Drever was Augustus Smith's cousin, heiress to the vast Dorrien fortune, engaged to his brother James. The small, intolerant Miss Drever – later Mrs Smith-Dorrien – refused to visit Scilly, and discouraged her children from so doing, lest she or they somehow absorb Augustus's moral toxins.

Augustus Smith's cottages were sturdy, simple, and built with raised floors, damp courses, and porches to stop the weather getting into the living rooms. This one, Cliff on Tresco, was the residence of Mary Pender, mother of his children. In the centre are the mill and the farm.

Lady Sophia Tower, Augustus Smith's lifelong friend and correspondent, whose daughter married T.A. Dorrien Smith, Augustus Smith's heir. She was a woman of formidable intelligence and immense kindness, rumoured to have taken a cold bath every morning of her long life.

A woman not affected by Mrs Smith-Dorrien's bourgeois scruples was Lady Sophia Tower, whose lengthy correspondence with Augustus began in the mid-1840s. Lady Sophia was a Hertfordshire neighbour. She had married the perfectly harmless Christopher Tower, a gentleman of leisure who spent much of his life moving from European spa to European spa taking very good care of his already robust health. Reading their letters, it is hard to avoid the conclusion that she must sometimes have wished she had married Augustus.

It is also tempting to wonder whether Augustus wished he had married her. Certainly he was a profoundly unconventional man, and his intellectual closeness to Lady Sophia, coupled with his physical closeness to Mary Pender and her successor, could almost be said to add up to a form of polygamy. But it is through his letters to her, preserved with hagiological zeal after his death, that his private and semi-private thoughts are revealed. They contain wide discussions of politics ecclesiastical and secular, personalities and London gossip, that kept his mind and his house-parties buzzing thirty miles west of Land's End. Lady Sophia was a friend and confidante to him for the best part of thirty years – thirty years brilliant and pleasurable, but also years of struggle against official self-interest and reaction.

Augustus emerges as a man quite at ease with himself and his friends, though prone to bursts of despair at the stupidities of Mrs Grundys about his private life. He had always had a taste for wildness, in ideas as well as places. He had a great deal of work to do against very large odds. The wildness of Scilly and the remoteness of its position made tasks that would have been daunting on the mainland positively Herculean. The next of these Herculean labours was the securing for Scilly of a decent postal service.

This had nothing to do with the sending of holiday postcards. In the age of sail, ships would arrive suddenly and without warning out of the wastes of the Atlantic, wishing to know to which European port they should carry their cargoes[8]. During the early years of Augustus Smith's tenure, there was no postal service. Augustus complained that this was crippling the islands' usefulness as a port, preventing 'up to 200 ships' at a time communicating with their owners. The

---

8. The primary purpose of Marconi's new radio, whose first installation was sixty years later on the Lizard, was to notify ship owners of the arrival of their vessels in the Channel.

The *Ariadne*, fifty-two tons, last sailing packet on the Scilly run. She had once been a gentleman's yacht. Augustus Smith liked her because of the extreme comfort of the bunk in the captain's cabin; and also because she was a lovely boat to windward. She was sold out of the ferry service in 1858.

Handbill for the *Lionesse*, Captain Frank Tregarthen, the *Ariadne*'s predecessor. Note the mailbag clause, which proved the undoing of Mr Cresswell's underhand stratagem with the nauseated Colenzo.

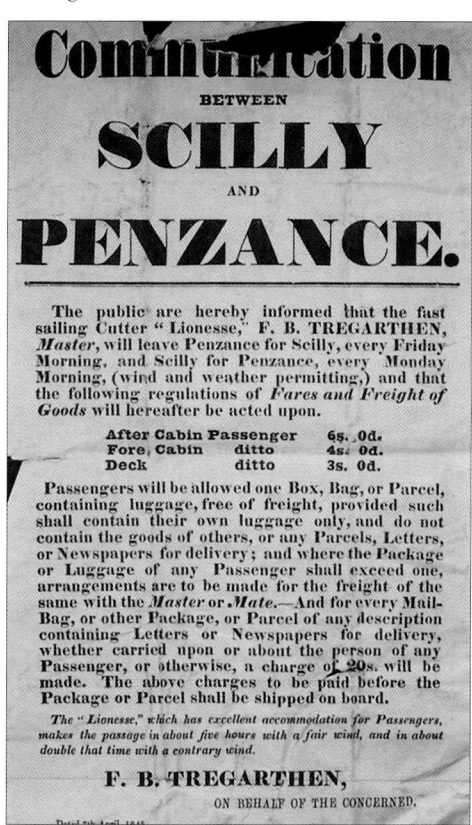

Post Office refused to supply a service, claiming that the volume of mail did not justify spending £100 a year on a contract with the St Mary's Shipping Company.

Augustus thought this was nonsense, and as usual said so. He wrote to the local Post Office functionaries, pointing out that the volume of mail was small because the Post Office provided a wretched service, and that many letters were therefore sent privately. Having thus offended official self-importance, he then wrote over the heads of the local men to Colonel Maberley, Secretary of the Post Office. Maberley got the Admiralty to supply a seaworthy packet. A service began and continued for three years.

But the local bureaucrats had not forgiven Mr Smith, either for pointing out their incompetence or for going over their heads.

This became evident when a Mr Cresswell was appointed Post Office Surveyor in the West. This was a position which vested in its holder great authority and virtually no accountability – not a combination calculated to appeal to Augustus Smith's instincts. Cresswell rejected the St Mary's Shipping Company's bid to carry the mail for £52 a year, sought other tenders, and received only one, from the St Mary's Shipping Company, now asking for £100 a year. Augustus held his peace, much amused. Cresswell got annoyed. Another tenderer turned up, was accused by Cresswell of being a stooge of the St Mary's Shipping

47

Company, and demanded that he withdraw the allegation. The arguments took on a strident, even shrill, quality.

Here Augustus stepped in, seeking to soothe the parties but ill-equipped to do so by his loathing of the Cresswells of this world. Succumbing to an attack of frankness, he accused the Post Office of double dealing. Cresswell claimed that the mail problems were the fault of the Shipping Company, and refused to open a money order office on St Mary's on the (unsupported) grounds that whoever ran it was likely to become a career embezzler if he was not one already. Augustus, who had been making calculations of his own, produced a set of true and correct figures demonstrating that Cresswell was a liar, and in an early example of a public-private partnership offered to subsidise the service. Meanwhile he prepared a memorial for Parliament advertising to a fascinated public Cresswell's false accounting and general perfidy. The St Mary's Shipping Company got the contract.

In 1843 Mr Cresswell declared open war. He terminated the (now £200-a-year) contract with the St Mary's Shipping Company and chartered a mail boat from the Admiralty 'to bring Mr Smith to his senses.' The Admiralty supplied mail transport for the summer (but not the winter, claiming it would be 'dangerous') and sent Mr Cresswell a bill for £1335.19.4d.

Cresswell sank into a deep sulk. He entirely refused to employ the Shipping Company, still the only tenderers. Instead he hired a stooge, one Colenzo, a Penzance glazier with a grudge against Augustus. Colenzo's job was to smuggle the Scilly mail to the islands via the packet, posing as a private citizen. On his first trip he was sick all over the mailbag and was spotted by the captain of the packet, who charged him the standard 20/- for carrying a mailbag, plus his 12/- return fare and two shillings boat hire to the quay. This, added to the £75 p.a. salary agreed with Cresswell, made him considerably more expensive than any previous tenderer, except the Admiralty. You could hear Scilly laughing from the mainland.

Not long after this in 1846, Lord St. Germans, a Cornish peer and a friend of Augustus, became Postmaster General. The letters began to flow, and Mr Cresswell was heard from no more. Mr Smith had won.

* * *

Summer holidays on Scilly in the 1840s would be recognizable now. Obviously, there would be sun, sand and crystal sea. There were watercolours instead of photographs, sails and oars instead of outboards. Man was the divinely appointed

ABOVE *Déjeuner sur l'herbe*, northeast of Tresco Abbey across the Pool. The painter was Dr Moyle of St Mary's – friend and sometimes confidant of Augustus Smith, talented and popular physician and co-founder of the Scilly Institute, dedicated to public education and enlightenment. Dr Moyle has taken the usual painterly liberties with the landscape. Augustus Smith is fourth from the left, talking to an Admiral. Batchelor the butler is uncorking wine. In the background, *Ariadne* is heading up-channel for St Mary's.

LEFT Sociable climbing on the Punch Bowl Rock, St Agnes.

RIGHT The art of picnicking reaches its highest expression at Scilly. Here, top hats are being worn by lunchers awaiting the arrival of the ladies under their sail on Tean.

BELOW. . . while round the corner, cooks and boatmen get the fire going.

Sightseers by the dark mouth of Piper's Hole, wondering whether they can face the slippery boulders and the awful chill of the subterranean pool.

pinnacle of creation, nature put there for his convenience. Or so Christopher Tower and other sporting Abbey guests seemed to think, as they shot birds prior to watching them. Augustus was less interested in slaughter than in conversation. Picnics were conducted on an heroic scale, with dining-tables and chairs arranged under sails slung from rocks, and battalions of staff striving over cauldrons and pulling broadsides of corks from batteries of bottles. Visits to the off-islands were made under sail or oar in one of Augustus's fleet. On calm days, small boats slid over the glassy flats, spearing turbot – two at a time, often, as the male turbot rises to the surface with the harpooned female, and can be easily gaffed. To the west, the horizon was still empty, though on a calm evening a thread of smoke would be rising from Rosevear, where the builders of the first Bishop lighthouse had their encampment.

This lighthouse, while of great benefit to mariners, was something of a stone in Augustus Smith's shoe. Trinity House, the body responsible for pilotage and seamarks in English water, was founded in the time of Henry VIII. It was powerful, capricious and unaccountable. In Augustus's view it was also wasteful, self-interested, run by seagoing dinosaurs known as Elder Brethren and staffed by ruffians. He had already made clear his views about an early plan by Trinity House to site the light marking Scilly's Western rocks on Rosevear, in the heart of those rocks rather than on their western margin. And when Trinity House decided that the Bishop Rock, most westerly of Scilly, was indeed the right spot, Augustus was forthrightly sceptical about the design – a sort of iron tripod surmounted by a lantern, the theory being that the waves would wash through the legs, rather than spend their titanic force on a stone tower.

These views did not endear him to the Elder Brethren. Nor did his forcefully-expressed opinions on their employment policies. Trinity House believed in employing men as young as sixteen to run their lights, imprisoning them for three months at a stretch in stone towers that stank of paraffin and in which there was no chance of exercise. Augustus suggested that such berths would be better filled by retired seamen with experience of the maritime life. The Elder Brethren instantly rejected some delightful houses that he had built on Tresco for the keepers of the Seven Stones Lightship, moving them instead to Penzance, an infinitely less convenient base. This

ABOVE The first Bishop Rock light. Trinity House considered that the construction – a slender iron latticework supporting a central lantern – would stand a good chance of surviving the enormous waves prevalent hereabouts. Augustus Smith did not agree, and made no secret of the fact. He was proved right when the entire structure vanished during a gale, happily without loss of life.

LEFT The lighthouse-builders' encampment on Rosevear, a beautiful but soil-free island in the Western Rocks. The men grew lettuces in deposits of rotten seaweed and shag guano left in the cracks between boulders.

View from Tresco Abbey of the Royal Squadron anchored near Nut Rock in 1847. The Royal Standard flies from the masthead of the Royal Yacht *Victoria and Albert*. St Agnes Lighthouse looms in the background haze.

was visibly (and rather satisfactorily) an act of spite by the Brethren. Augustus was further vindicated when during a fearsome gale in the winter of 1849-50 the iron Bishop light vanished, without loss of life but with great loss of face to Nicholas Douglass, its Northumbrian designer (and father of James Douglass, architect of the granite Bishop Rock light which stands to this day).

In the midst of the holidays and feuds came an event that partook a little of each. On August 13th 1847, the Royal Yacht, with the Queen and Prince Albert on board and escorted by several warships, dropped anchor in St Mary's Roads. The Royal party was en route for Balmoral, and had only paused at Scilly because their trip had been disrupted by fog. Augustus instantly arranged a loyal reception. The entire population of St Mary's turned out to welcome the Royal party onto the quay. There was Mr Smith at the head of a reception committee of magistrates and clergy. There were principal tenants carrying white wands with which to hold back the uncontrollably eager populace (which in the event behaved itself with the usual impeccable Scillonian manners). The Queen, who had been vilely seasick and was dressed in black, proceeded to the Garrison, stood on a chair so she could see over the wall, and made jokes about her height, at which everyone laughed dutifully. Augustus's coachman then took the Royal party on a short tour of the island. Possibly stricken with nerves, the coachee managed to take a wrong turning from the very few available, and started driving down the excessively steep Garrison Hill. The Queen and Prince Albert bailed out in a panic, and walked back to the quay in something of a tizz. The people lining the route in hope of a Royal drive-by had to content themselves with a sight of the Royal barge rowing swiftly away, Prince Albert muttering darkly in the stern sheets. The Royal squadron sailed for Milford Haven that night, while festive bonfires twinkled from the islands.

Mr Smith had done his frank and open best to make his sovereign feel at home. It may have worked for the Queen, but the consort had not been impressed. Prince Albert was an improving landlord, but in the German despotic tradition. Benthamism, stressing the power of the individual to rise in society through his own efforts, seemed to him to be perilously close to Socialism. Prince Albert's notion of improvement was a top-down affair, in which the wise prince bestowed upon his

The Royal barge approaches the steps in the New Pier (quay) at St Mary's. Augustus Smith, builder of the quay, is on the right, wearing his trademark telescope and doffing his hat.

St Mary's Pier was not the only quay Augustus Smith built. This picture gives a sample of his works on Tresco, public as well as private. The quay and slipway exist pretty much unchanged to this day. The cottages, built and repaired by Augustus, are snug, light and wholesome. On the right is the farm.

grateful subjects the benisons of his God-given wisdom. It is hard to avoid the conclusion that Augustus Smith thought he was a puppy.

The situation had not been improved by the Duchy of Cornwall's bad behaviour over the Scilly lease. As Lord Warden of the Duchy, Prince Albert was certainly aware that Augustus's negotiations for the consolidation of his lease on the islands had reached an impasse. Augustus wished for the Duchy's assurance that the huge amounts of work and money he had poured into Scilly could be enjoyed by his heirs. For this purpose he needed to renegotiate a bulletproof modern lease to replace the previous model, which was to run for the term of ninety-nine years or three specified lives, whichever was the shorter. This lease had been dependent on the goodwill of both parties for its success. Duchy goodwill had lately been conspicuous by its absence, and not only towards Augustus Smith, Duchy tenants in Penzance having been subjected to an opportunistic demand for £800. Augustus and his fellow tenants particularly resented the Duchy's habit of moving the goalposts when under pressure. As a body unaccountable to

Parliament and operating under a bizarre clutch of medieval statutes, this was easy for it to do, and impossible for tenants to combat.

So as Prince Albert visited Scilly, he would have had fresh in his mind Augustus Smith's memorial entitled *Thirteen Years' Stewardship of the Isles of Scilly*, addressed to Prince Albert and later published. In this, Augustus pointed out the change in relations with the Duchy that had taken place since the death of King William. He further declared that unless the Duchy granted him more secure tenure, he would abandon all improvements not specified in the lease. In the process of making these excellent but abrasive debating points, Augustus also succeeded in quoting back at Prince Albert a speech the Prince had made. In this, he had expressed his 'feeling of sympathy and interest for that class of our community who have most of the toil and fewest of the enjoyments of the world.' The Prince had gone on to summarise the wonderful effect on these toilers of 'influential people, who . . . might be able to act the part of a friend to those who required advice and assistance,' and advocate to 'particular schemes of social

New Grimsby Quay. The principal change to this structure since Augustus Smith's day has been the addition of a complex of railings for the preservation of yachtsmen returning from the New Inn.

55

The entrance to Tresco Abbey from the Abbey Drive. Hydrangeas were a popular Cornish flower by now, and shooting a popular pastime. Augustus Smith was a dachshund enthusiast.

improvement.' In the light of these remarks, the Duchy's behaviour left the Prince looking like a considerable hypocrite – particularly as in the view of the Duchy the rents of Smith tenants were 'ridiculously low.'

Naturally, Augustus had in his good nature made the same miscalculation as with Trinity House and the Post Office. His memorial, reliant on plain speaking and rational argument, was more likely to infuriate than persuade the courtiers who interposed themselves between Prince and people. But Augustus was not bothered about ruffling people's feelings. As far as he was concerned, he had told the truth and acted fairly. Now it was the Duchy's turn. It was one of the flaws in his personality that he could not conceive of people acting in any other way.

He now decided to extend his influence beyond the islands. A Parliamentary vacancy presented itself at Truro. Augustus, espousing the Liberal interest, set himself to fill it.

FOUR

The Golden Age

During the late 1840s and early 1850s, Augustus Smith increased in girth and in understanding of the islands. According to folklore, the young men of St Agnes had once lashed him into a sail and pegged him out below the high water mark to drown, repenting only at the last moment. There was no question of this kind of carry-on now. Mr Smith and the Scillonians were on a footing. The Smith eye, assisted by the telescope invariably slung about his body, had attained a practically supernatural acuteness. In 1849, for instance, he transferred himself for a month to St Agnes, to supervise the building of roads and schools. He took up residence in the parsonage, there being no parson at that moment[9]. Close by, he found a Mr Mortimer building a pigsty with stones that exactly fitted certain holes in Augustus's new-built walls, and instructed him at a range of several hundred yards to restore the status quo.

The whimsies multiplied, to the delight of his house guests. Samson was finally depopulated in 1855 after an unpleasant incident in which the notorious witch known as the Widow Webber temporarily turned the Proprietor's bones to lead, rendering him incapable of locomotion. The Webbers were replaced with black rabbits, a pleasing contrast to those installed on Tean. Mr Rodd, the Proprietor's ornithological

---

[9]. Unmarried Scilly parsons tended to 'go mad or get into mischief'. Married ones fell into deep despair. Typically, both kinds lasted a year or two at most.

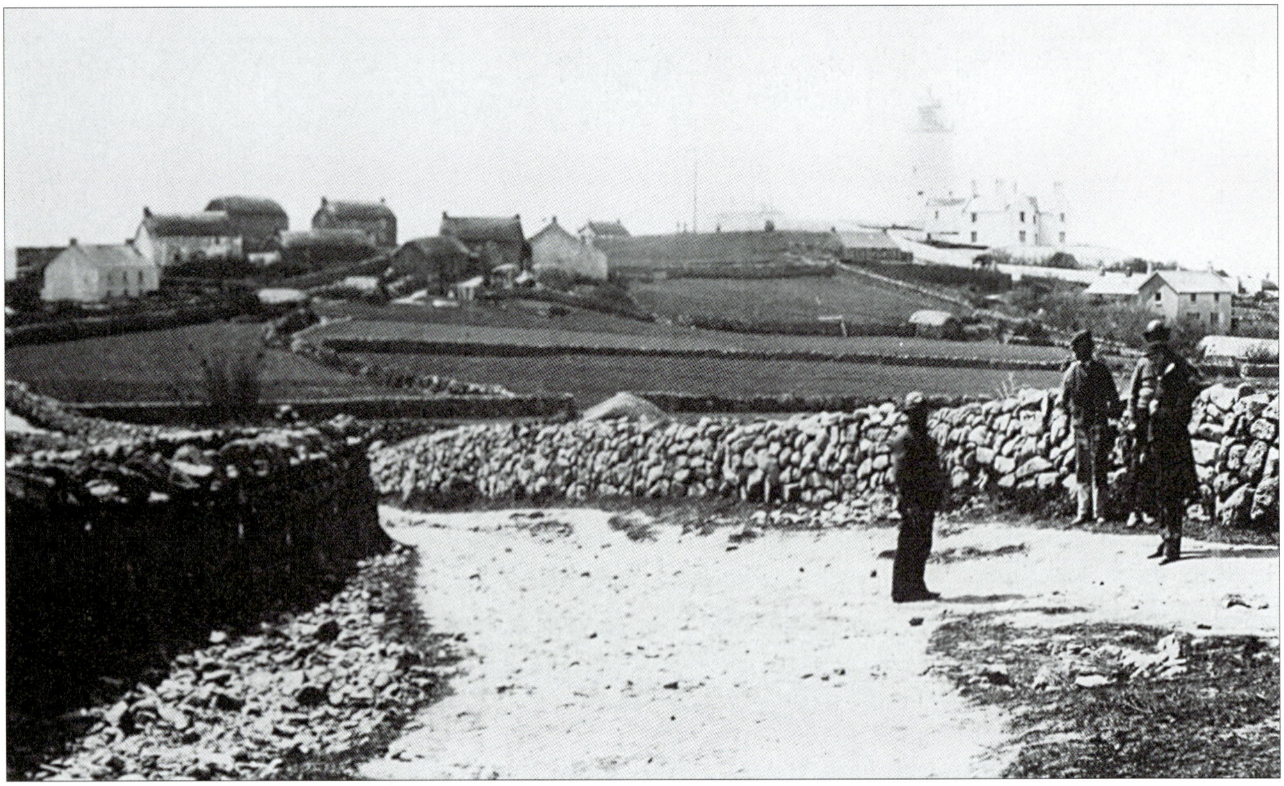

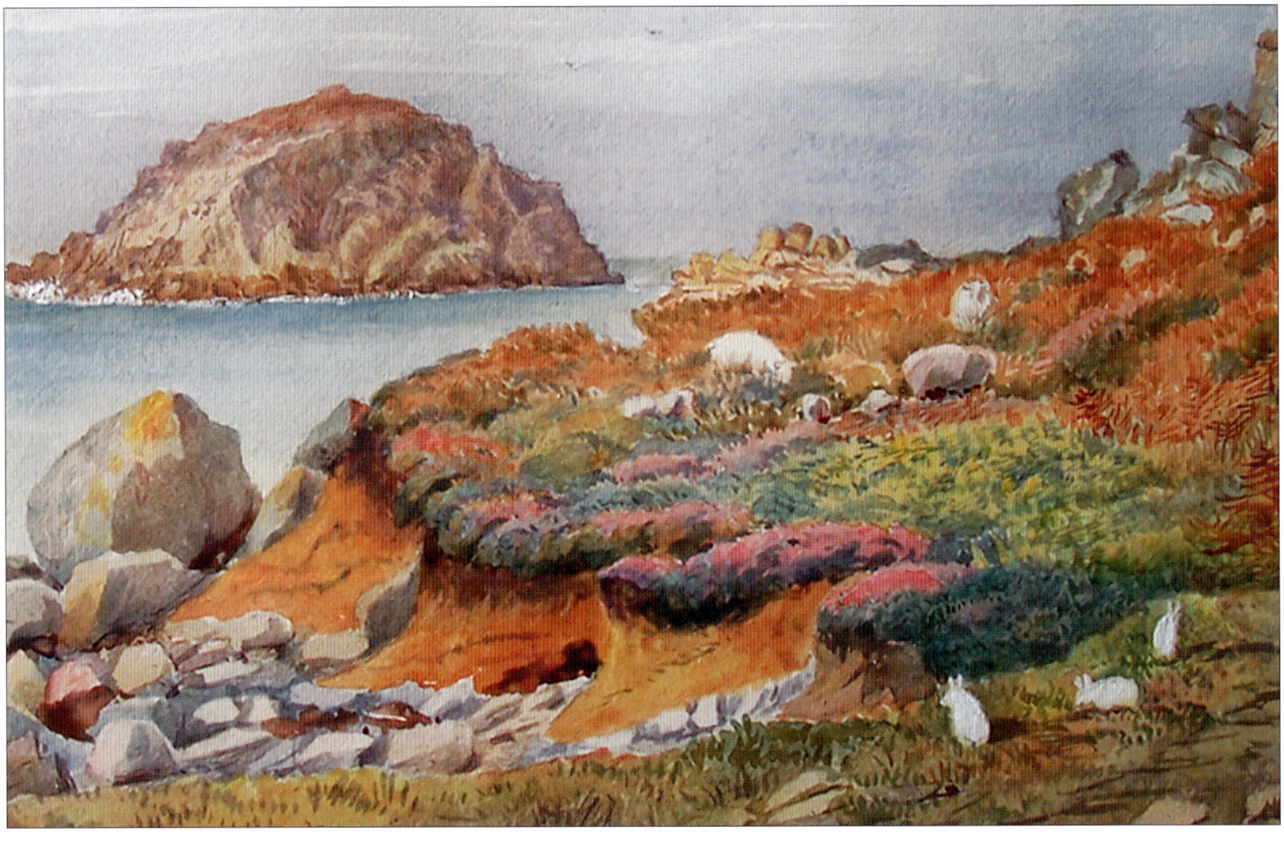

friend, secured specimens of the Scops owl and the night heron, but was frustrated in his attempts to batter stormy petrels out of the sky with an oar. Augustus's botanical enthusiasm waxed, and his correspondence with Sir William Hooker of Kew grew temporarily warm, despite the failure of clumpy Tupac grass from the Falklands to grow on Scilly. The two men hoped it would do better in the Orkneys (it did not). Wind-hardy Falkland Veronicas did much better. Augustus's guests, characters with mentalities as busy as their host's, anthropologised and botanised in the Victorian manner. The people of the islands, they concluded, had the following characteristics: the inhabitants of St Martins were tall and thin, thanks to their descent from Vikings. Those of St Agnes were short, stout and dark. Their supposed descent from Barbary Corsairs, or alternatively the crews of a wrecked Armada galleon, had left them with the sobriquet of Turks or Bezibezeeks. The inhabitants of Bryher were known as Thorns, and those of Tresco as Caterpillars, apparently because of their silhouettes when carrying case-bottles of smuggled brandy across the Downs on their backs.

The soap opera continued. In 1850 the magistrates fined various people for burning figures on poles during the usual early-May larks. One of them, who pleaded not guilty, bore the name of Horatio Nelson[10]. This tearaway later got two months in the house of correction for stealing turnips, and was

ABOVE The launch of the topsail schooner *Nundeeps*, built for the Argentine hoof-and-hide – glue – trade by the Penders. The *Nundeeps* was one of many small but weatherly ships owned, built and fitted out on Scilly.

OPPOSITE PAGE TOP The throbbing hub of St Agnes after one of Augustus Smith's visits. The granite hedges have been recently rebuilt, and the houses are in a high state of maintenance.

OPPOSITE PAGE BOTTOM As part of the amenities of the new Scilly, Augustus Smith introduced rabbits of various colours to various islands. It is hard to be sure which colours went where. Black rabbits were certainly to be found on Samson until fairly recent times, and more were apparently settled on St Helens. Judging by this picture, the ones he put on nearby Tean were white.

10. This is thought to be the same Horatio Nelson who in later life became the St Mary's policeman.

Pilot boats – cutter-rigged like *Pettifox*, seen here – patrolled the far Western Approaches, looking for ships to take up-Channel. Six- or seven-oared gigs raced to place pilots on ships closer to the islands. In the days before the lifeboat service, gigs' crews performed acts of astonishing heroism, often unrewarded, to rescue seamen in distress.

OPPOSITE PAGE Frontispiece of Rev I.W. North's *A Week in the Isles of Scilly*, illuminated by Lady Sophia Tower. Augustus Smith at his most Imperial – surmounted by his crest, underslung by his Masonic insignia, and framed in the products of his empire.

fined for riding a horse furiously through Hugh Town.

The shipping industry was now in decline after six years of unparalleled prosperity. The arrival of steam was blamed. Dr. Carne, a natural philosopher collecting for the museum in Oxford brought to the Abbey evenings 'the real German backgammon.' The Wizard of the North, a travelling conjuror, was kidnapped to perform his wonders in the schoolroom. There were vulgar stories, noted in Augustus's commonplace book: 'As a gentleman and lady were walking along a street a labourer very offensively let off a tremendous rouser just as they were passing. The gentleman came back to do battle with the culprit, exclaiming, "How dare you, Sir, let out that f---t before my wife?" "Before your wife?" answered the fellow. "Had I known she was going to f---t, I would have waited for her."' Boom boom.

The autumn was a succession of brilliant days, turbot, red mullet, and startlingly red guernsey lilies – somewhere between an agapanthus and a nerine – that Augustus had brought back from the Channel Islands. In November, the Duchy was at it again in 'the spirit of trick and deception which animates the main springs, and which they consider as being very *diplomatic*.' Early the following year, Augustus was doing the kind of practical work he liked, allocating shares in £2500 paid as salvage for the wreck of the *San Giorgio*, towed in from 50 miles west of the Bishop by seventeen pilot cutters sailing in line ahead. He was also writing in praise of the Hungarian patriot Kossuth, dictator of Hungary, who had thrown out the Austrian oppressor – 'though I care little about him . . . but I like the faithless despots of Europe to be made to understand what . . . England thinks of them.' The faithless despots of the Duchy were never far from his mind.

AUGUSTUS SMITH ESQ^R

An unknown girl hobnobbing with a goose. Augustus Smith loathed the crinoline, and spoke with deep respect of a yachtload of Godolphin girls who came to visit. They eschewed boots, caught dozens of fish, swam at every opportunity without benefit of bathing-machines, and horrified his boatmen by the vigour and expertise of their rowing. This kind of behaviour later became the hallmark of Tresco femininity.

But Augustus Smith was not one to knuckle under. He directed his attention elsewhere, busying himself with the shelter belts, where he was replacing the deciduous trees with evergreens, particularly *Cupressus macrocarpa* (the Monterey pine, *pinus radiata*, which eventually consolidated the shelter belts, was not planted until the next generation of Smiths had taken over Scilly). Tresco White Dorkings, Muscovy ducks and Egyptian Geese swept the board at the Penzance Poultry Show got up by his ornithological friend Rodd. The Lord Proprietor also began to make himself pleasant to the electors of Truro, and took a long lease on 1, Eaton Square, London, handy for the Palace of Westminster, which pending his election he let to Lady Sophia Tower and her family at a small rent, contingent on her help with the decorations. 'You may indulge in flowers, arabesque, simple spots, seaweed, leopard skins, or anything you please as to pattern,' he wrote. Lady Sophia, knowing Augustus's taste for brilliance and exoticism, obliged with acres of geraniums.

The election did not turn out as Augustus had hoped. He lost by eight votes, thanks to his opponents' judicious crookery. In the autumn, fierce gales skittled trees and entirely demolished the bathing machine lashed with stout ropes into a gulch in the dunes behind Bathing House Beach. Augustus, now constantly in touch with his agent in Truro, put down a marker for the next election, which (given the gossip he now heard on his trips to London) could not be long in coming.

In the early autumn of 1853 he sought a change of air in Ireland, where he stayed as so often with a pioneering landlord – in this case George Clive, of the celebrated Herefordshire family of tree-planters and estate improvers. Clive had bought 40,000 acres of bog and mountain, 'the perfection of wildness,' which under his untypically benevolent ownership produced a good return on investment, even in those immediately post-famine days. This precipitated a *cri de coeur*: 'Could I but slip my moorings at Scilly with the prospects before me, as the reward for all my exertions and outlays through that damned Duchy, I should not hesitate even now to pitch my home somewhere here.'

Since the misbehaviour of the Duchy and his failure with the electors of Truro, Augustus seemed for a moment at sixes and sevens. On the one hand, he watched with horror as an emigrant ship put in at Scilly full of 600 victims of the Highland clearances 'leaky, the owners being . . . rogues.' Compelled to take on a doctor, the ship took on a quack and vanished over the horizon. On the other hand, things were stirring in Berkhamstead. The second Lord Brownlow, Lady Sophia Tower's nephew, was litigating to inherit Ashridge, an estate close to Ashlyns. Brownlow was a man with no chin and a mother of boundless ambition. Augustus, always fascinated by questions of landowning, followed the drowsy court proceedings with a mixture of eagerness and irony, beguiling particularly dull sections by writing letters. One of these requested plants from Kew.

This was a missive so ill-calculated that it can only have been the product of a mind dulled by incipient sleep. It combined a humble request for plants with far from humble instructions about how the request should be granted. Arrogant to begin with, it seems to have caught the elderly Director on a bad day. The resultant blast, in which Sir William told Mr Smith to go and buy his plants from nurseries like everybody else, terminated relations between Tresco and Kew for the next twelve years. Augustus wrote a letter of apology and turned to nurseries like Treseders of Moresk, whose programme of Australasian introductions had developed to the point where it could fulfil many of his needs. There were other consolations, in the shape of an ostrich that had shown up on a ship from Rio and been kidnapped for the garden. It was soon joined by others. Ostrich eggs appeared on the Abbey breakfast menu.

The new election was not as quick in coming as Smith had hoped. He found himself trapped and frustrated. He complained with the full passion of his larger-than-life nature that the Duchy was making him impotent at Scilly, and his lack of public position was making him powerless in public life. The Crimean War juddered into existence, exposing incompetence in the British officer corps and corruption in the civil service.

Lord Brownlow, posing perhaps unwisely in profile. He was a man much under the influence of his mother. This powerful woman insisted that he was delicate, and that he should therefore spend the winters in Madeira. On his visits he was accompanied by several sheep and a shepherd, to ensure a steady supply of mutton chops of the correct tenderness.

Augustus Smith's larger ornamental garden fauna.

Augustus raged against both, and against Prince Albert, whose appeasing views on the war seemed more calculated to fulfil the aims of the Russian enemy than of the British and their allies. His sister Fanny's husband, Major le Marchant, sent back from the front horror stories about cholera in the ranks, wormy equipment, muddle and disorder. Augustus thought the charge of the Light Brigade 'disastrous'. He loathed and despised Leopold of the Belgians, Queen Victoria's whoremongering uncle, who ran the Congo as his personal estate. He despised the German princelings whom he suspected of wishing to promote a squalid and humiliating peace. Time spent in London recalled to him the sense of suffocation that had driven him away from Berkhamstead as a young man. Though he loved Ashlyns, he said 'I only wish I could lift it up and put it down near the sea, two hundred miles from London and free from a genteel neighbourhood.' He spoke fondly of its garden and 'my mother, to whom [it] chiefly owes its form and arrangement, and with which my boyhood is identified.' Happiness lay on Scilly.

Despite the cooling of relations with Kew, Augustus Smith's own garden was approaching a high state of perfection, with the erection of a granite replica of the Malakoff redoubt, part of the eastern defences of Sebastopol, at the summit of the East rockery, crowned with chevaux-de-frise of Aloes. A hoity-toity gardener called Spriggins departed after a short tenure, and another called Chivers arrived. Chivers, a man of huge skill and intelligence, was to become one of the principal builders of the Tresco garden. 'Oh, the difference between a sharp and a blunt tool, a head and a blockhead!' cried the Lord Proprietor. Another excitement was a visit from the great novelist Wilkie Collins in the *Tomtit*, a yacht of minute size. Collins greatly admired Scilly, praising the kindness, skill and volubility of the people. He disapproved of the fact they never opened windows – to which he attributed the very high rate of consumption in the islands, where it was indeed the chief cause of death. As to Mr Smith, Collins said: 'he has reformed and taught [the islanders]; and there is now, probably, no place in England where the direr hardships of poverty are so little known as in the Scilly Islands.'

Augustus himself was delighted to meet the famous author, whose novels he found tosh but unputdownable. He felt himself rather attuned to the media this year. His lecture on the Crimea (complete with rock samples) had been a huge success on St Mary's, and he was repeating it at the Truro Institute.

His friend Pendarves had died, and left him as trustee of the estate. The heir was a Somerset youth called William Cole Wood. In one of those nineteenth century moves that is the despair of genealogists and to which the descendants of Augustus Smith were not immune[11], the heir changed his name to Pendarves. His father was both very rich and very grasping, so Augustus's friend, Tryphena, young Pendarves' great-aunt, made sure that the youth spent the summer as part of the throng at Tresco Abbey. In later years he became the closest thing Augustus ever had to a son, receiving much kindness, as well as instruction in the management of land, houses and people. Frustratingly, no letters survive, and Pendarves itself, with its famous garden and its model estate village, has been swamped by the grim tide of Camborne.

11. The present lessee of Tresco, Augustus Smith's great-great-nephew, bears the surname Smith Dorrien Smith. Happily, the first Smith is silent.

Tresco Abbey from the Penzance Road, showing the East Rockery, topped by the rocks of the Malakoff Redoubt. It was through this rockery that a discreet path ran to Augustus Smith's rooms on the ground floor of the gable to the left of the flowering Agave.

St Mary's in 2004 – the picture of a thriving island. The prosperity begun under Augustus Smith continues to the present day.

By early 1857, Sir Charles Lemon had retired, and was urging his friend (and fellow mason) Augustus Smith to stand as Member for Cornwall. Augustus refused, on the grounds of 'my very recent connection with the country and my total want of family connection with it' – though possibly he did not fancy another humiliating knockback, as at Truro previously. But in March, he agreed to stand again as a Liberal in Truro, and after vigorous canvassing was returned as an MP.

Scilly was exceedingly proud of its entry onto the national stage. 160 people sat down to a grand dinner in the infant schoolroom on St Mary's. St Agnes threw a mighty tea drinking, illuminated with tar barrel bonfires[12]. Augustus

12. St Agnes, wildest of the off-islands, was inordinately keen on tar barrel bonfires, letting no opportunity for one slip by.

School treat at St Mary's in 1849. The children throng the school grounds, and a brand new Scilly-built topsail schooner rejoices in the harbour. Everyone enjoyed themselves immensely, no one more so than Augustus Smith.

Augustus Smith in his garden by a Puya, with telescope and dachshund.

declared that 'the whole affair, so spontaneously taken up, has shown a very gratifying feeling on the part of the islanders.' There was a short space for satisfaction and the recovery from speechmaking of his throat, always a weak part of his anatomy. Then the letters began to arrive.

It is reasonable to suspect that there were parts of being an MP that Augustus did not much enjoy. On Scilly he was a benevolent dictator, beholden to no-one. As MP for Truro he was public property. At a time when there was no such concept as sleaze, this meant a lot of dealing with importunate constituents who made no bones about the fact that Mr Smith's compliance was the condition of their further support. Among these were a Mr Wroath, who offered his vote in exchange for Augustus getting him a job in the customs (in an earlier attempt at the entry exam, Mr Wroath had scored 208 marks out of 1300, including 0 out 150 for Geography, 1 out of 150 for History, and 0 out of 200 for Bookkeeping). A Josiah Randall in his first paragraph acknowledged Augustus's gift of Samuel Smiles' *Self-Help* to the Truro Institute. In the second he made a surprising departure from the Smiles doctrine, asking Augustus's influence for a weedy nephew who had 'walked down self-denial street all his days.' God, observed Mr Randall (departing even further from Smiles) tempers the wind to the shorn lamb.

At home during the summer, Augustus Smith was receiving political visitors of a more rarified type. There was the historian J.A. Froude, a mandarin entity who allowed as how he was impressed by what a man of 'no extraordinary abilities but with a strong will and a resolute purpose to do good' could achieve. Froude called Augustus Smith a king on a small scale. But he was impressed that he used his authority not for himself but for the good of his subjects, took no profit, had no luxuries but his garden, and ploughed the estate rents back for the welfare of the tenants. He was held to be an ogre, but respected with it.

John Stuart Mill, the great Utilitarian moral philosopher and the philosophical heir of Augustus's guru Jeremy Bentham, was less impressed. He considered that despite Augustus's defiance of autocracy, he had himself become an autocrat. 'I detest paternal government,' he said. Augustus seems to have paid no attention. By this time he was a burly and grizzled fifty-three-year-old, immersed in the doings of his islands and his constituency, a practical landlord and politician, more interested in the construction of the Top Terrace in the garden than the quiddities of moral philosophers.

As always, 'practical' was Augustus Smith's watchword. He was a good constituency member, but a half-hearted politician. His single-handed battles with the Duchy, Trinity House and the Post Office had not been good training for a tyro MP, expected to trot meekly through the lobby indicated by the Liberal whips. When away from London he begged Lady Sophia for gossip, preferably true, but false if no other kind was available. But when he was in London, he found the shifting alliances of party politics more than he could stomach. 'I am very slow in forming new friendships; but pride myself on an obstinate adherence to those of tried continuance.'

Augustus Smith poses with his masons and carpenters outside the front door of Tresco Abbey. Helping him examine the plans is the talented Chudleigh, his friend and chief mason.

ABOVE The Neptune Staircase in about 1860. It was finished in 1858. 'It will, I fear, rather make the lower alleys, especially the Long Walk, a little jealous,' said Augustus Smith.

RIGHT The same view today.

Soon after this, the Top Terrace was finished. Neptune, the figurehead of the tragic steamer *Thames*, wrecked with awful loss of life in the Western Rocks in 1841, was hoisted into 'his throne at the summit of the grand staircase.' In winter 1858, Augustus was enumerating the flowers of correas, fuchsias, genistas, sedums – what are now called aeoniums – with a smugness prefiguring that of Sir Thomas Hanbury at La Mortola, who copied the Tresco custom of every New Year's Day making a count of plants flowering. Scilly life continued, with its alarms and accidents and poor Townshend Boscawen, walking through he reedbed by the

Great Pool with his hands in his pockets when he tripped and fell on his face. A reed entered 'one or both eyes, which then went septic' until he pulled out the offending chunks.

But the world was changing, outside and inside Scilly. The Western rocks, long the abode of darkness, had since September 1858 been illuminated by the Bishop, 'very conspicuous between the two hills of Samson from these windows', a boon to mariners but a perpetual reminder of the perfidy of Trinity House. The following year, the sailing packet *Ariadne* was replaced by the paddle steamer *Little Western*, which connected with the Penzance-Plymouth railway, which had opened in May.

The regularity of the steamer had brought St Mary's closer to Penzance 'where London fashions are very fierce.' And the train . . . well, 'having started [from London] with the mails on Saturday evening, [Augustus] was breakfasting at the house of Rodd, the Penzance ornithologist, before the sun had reached its height.' Somewhat to Augustus's satisfaction, the off-islands did not yet share the benefits of the Steam Age, transport between them being by sail in a breeze and oar in a calm. But the process that ended in the clatter of helicopter rotors over the Tresco cricket pitch had begun.

Off Scilly, Augustus Smith was fully occupied with the steam age and its doings. There was an election – not a love-feast like

ABOVE The *Little Western*, which entered service on the Penzance-St Mary's run in 1859. Her name presumably sets her up in opposition to Brunel's enormous *Great Eastern*, launched in 1858. She was a boon to Augustus Smith and other commuters . . .

BELOW . . . though like all vessels plying the furious waters round Scilly, she was by no means immune to the vagaries of wind, weather and sea state.

71

View from the State Room into the Dining Room, mid-1860s. The conventional view of Victorians is of a gloomy generation, obsessed with darkness and mourning. The State Room is a bath of colour, illuminated by enormous windows. Note the eighteenth-century Chinese wallpaper, the plants in the (unheated) conservatory, and the sofa of many colours. The library, in great requisition during wet days and long evenings, had come from Ashlyns and Haresfoot, and was regularly updated by London booksellers.

the last one, but a slogging-match against John Vivian, a fellow Liberal of underhand tendencies. Augustus scraped home, and returned to his new circle at Westminster. His political friends were not the first in the land, whom he regarded as a slippery bunch of backstabbers. He tended to associate with radicals from the far corners of Britain – men like Mr Philipps of Williamston, with whom he stayed in the Pembrokeshire wilds, and the Dillwyns of Swansea, through whom he later became an habitué of the model town and astonishing Gothic house built by the Talbots at Margam.

It is never possible for a man to know when his life has

reached its peak. In the first couple of years of the 1860s, Scilly as a whole was in a state of prosperity, its populace cheerful, educated, and strangers to want. The Tresco garden was approaching its present form, already a magnet for tourists arriving by railway and *Little Western*. Augustus's new state rooms were built, decorated and in use. He had friends around him at Scilly, and a seat in the House. After lengthy negotiation, the Duchy of Cornwall had agreed on a lease whose terms made his position at least tenable. Prince Albert's death in 1861 removed a German despot, and the Prince of Wales' coming of age in 1863 would put in the

ABOVE LEFT The dining room at Tresco Abbey, remarkably little changed in 140 years.

ABOVE A detail from one of the Chinese 18th century wallpapers. They were brought back by Augustus Smith's merchant ancestors and he liked to think of them as his family portraits.

73

The Drawing Room at Tresco Abbey, about 1860. The wall panels were painted with Italian scenes by the family friend and amateur artist William Claridge. The distinctive bobbled frames are the work of an island wood-turner, using wreck timber. In the gradual evolution of Tresco Abbey, the verandah – visible outside the French window – has since been incorporated into the drawing room.

driver's seat the future Edward VII, a man whose more relaxed temperament was a better fit with Augustus Smith's Georgianism.

In the summer of 1862, the Towers paid their annual visit, accompanied by their children (known to Mr Smith as the Turrets). Mr Smith remained in the Abbey with Mr Rodd, the ornithologist and William Cole Pendarves, Mr Smith's young friend and almost-ward, now part of the bachelor circle. In his letters, Augustus was audibly proud of the settled and happy state of his Lilliputian world, the prosperity of his tenants, the cheerfulness of his house party, the beauty of his garden. Bright fires burned in the new staterooms. There was 'backgammon, draughts, tea and snooze', and more bad puns from the commonplace book. It was a golden age.

Gold is, of course, the colour of autumn.

Master Egerton Tower, son of Lady Sophia and a leading Turret, demonstrating the use of the stick in Her Ladyship's bedroom at Tresco Abbey.

FIVE

Emperor Smith

AUGUSTUS SMITH had now been in occupation of Scilly for nearly thirty years – a generation. He had given up his London house in Eaton Square, and thrown himself wholeheartedly into the popular Scillonian pastime of complaining about the hopelessness of the weather forecasts recently introduced by Admiral Fitzroy. He had by slow degrees metamorphosed from a chilly reformer into a proud Scillonian.

He was now fifty-five, and feeling every month of it, working eighteen-hour days on the welfare of the islands and the public finances. Some of his contemporaries seemed to have rather more free time than previously. He spoke with particular feeling about Lord Vernon, with whom he had been at Oxford. His Lordship arrived on Tresco with his wife in November 1861, and did not depart until April 1862, by which time Augustus was muttering darkly about importing kill-or-cure doctors, German bands, and the other appurtenances of sanatoria.

The more remote of his causes were beginning to slip from his grasp. In Berkhamstead, the governors of the Grammar School had converted Mr Smith's institution for the provision of a useful education into a gentrified establishment for the teaching of the Classics. He found this 'very stupid, very impolitic, and very unjust.' And in an age where steam was comprehensively replacing sail, he regretted the old days – not only because of the beauty of the ships, but because the ships once concentrated at Scilly by easterly breezes could now steam up the Channel regardless of wind direction. (Though it was noticeable that when the *Little Western* was being reboilered in Hayle, his nostalgia stopped well short of subjecting himself to becoming 'a marine victim in a pilot boat.')

ABOVE Tresco Abbey from the east, painted in the late 1860s. The gardens are visibly more mature, and the trees to the northeast of the house have grown up enough to mask the farm and the houses of New Grimsby.

BELOW LEFT A detail from a drawing showing the mackerel fleet leaving St Mary's. Hundreds of mackerel drivers – luggers, with big tan mainsails and mizzens sheeted to sprits – used to base themselves on Scilly during the mackerel season. The fish were caught in long drift-nets. There was perpetual rivalry between the Cornish boats and boats from the east coast, thanks to the latter's Godless habit of fishing on Sundays.

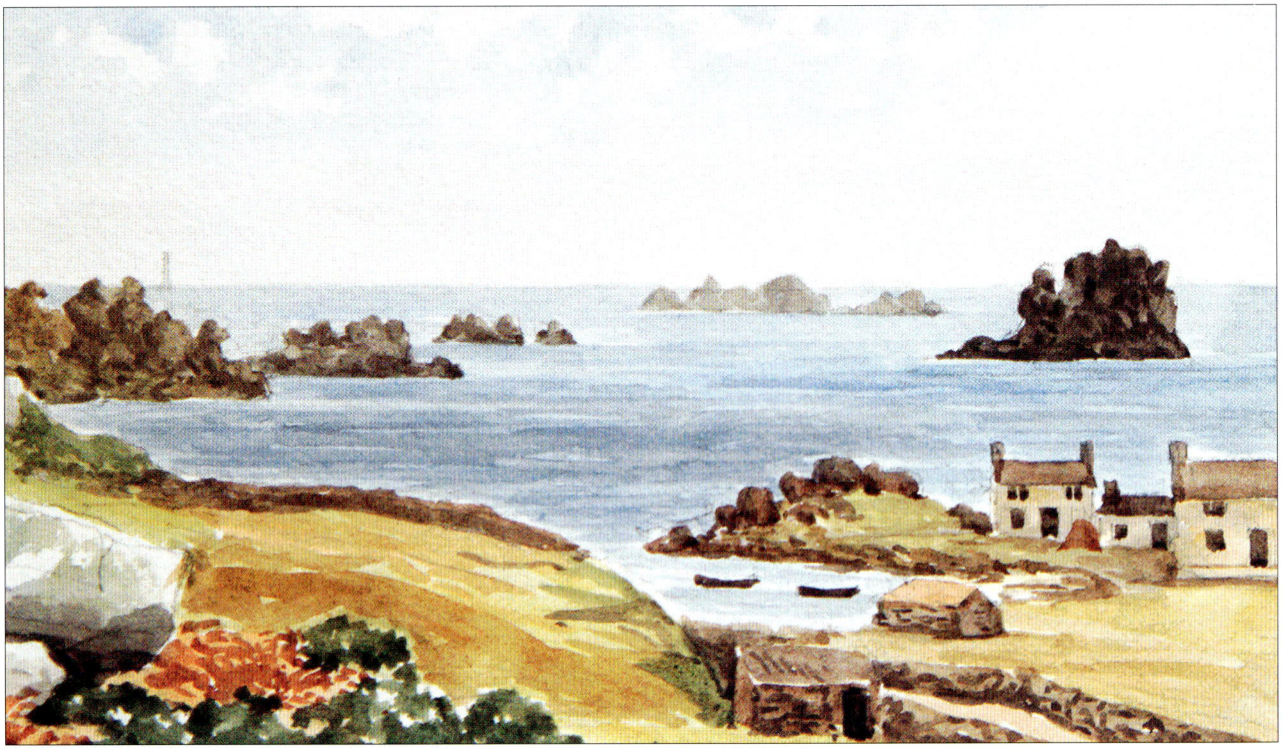

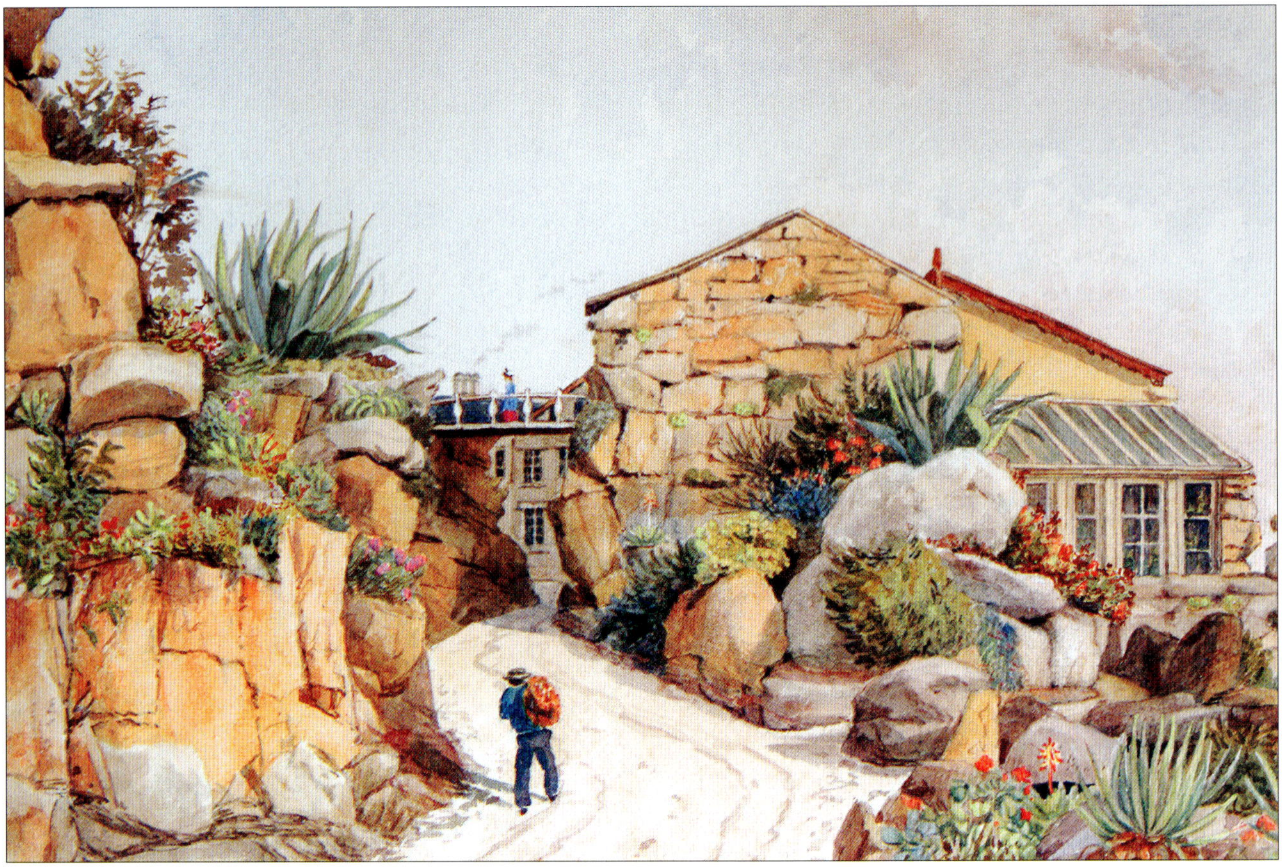

The spark of ambition still flared from time to time. In December 1864 he resolved to fight another election in Truro, ostensibly in the Liberal interest but actually 'entirely on my own stumps, and do my best to win, and if I don't, shall be content to spend a little more time on Scilly, particularly in Spring, when the cuckoos speechify to their constituents.' 'Mr Smith,' said the *Cornish Telegraph*, 'showed an unusual freedom from party ties.' This was a polite way of saying that Augustus had by now lost even the infinitesimal patience he had once had for trimming and compromise, and existed in a state of open and permanent revolt against party policy. He was known in Parliament as Scilly Smith – derided by the light-minded majority as an obsessive on the subject of foreshores, and respected by the more serious minority as a scourge of fudge and spin in Government accounts, at which he worried tirelessly.

His new flat in London, in Ashley Place off Victoria Street, was smaller and happily quieter than Eaton Square, decorated with a weekly basket of flowers sent up from Tresco. In it he pined for Scilly, and from it he sent Lady Sophia a draft of the address he intended to make announcing his retirement at the forthcoming election. In May 1865 he resigned – 'as glad as sorry to be out of Parliament' – though for the remainder of his life he suffered from surges of hankering for Westminster.

That spring, he had sent from Scilly to Covent Garden a box of narcissi – probably heavy-scented Scilly Whites and Soleil d'Or. These instantly sold for the astonishing sum of one pound. St Mary's growers, led by the redoubtable William Trevellick, were not slow to take note. The Scilly flower trade soon caught and overtook the lucrative early potato business. Flushed with this success – he never managed to make himself into much of a farmer – he visited Plymouth Agricultural Show on the way back to Scilly in July, but brought to the islands nothing more useful than a dose of pleurisy.

By the fourth of August, Scilly had cured him. He woke early, rose from his bed, roared for Batchelor, his butler, and caused a gig with a pilot to be sent into the fog off the Eastern Islands. At breakfast time a yacht materialised from the grey cotton wool, anchored by Nut Rock, and sent a boat to Carn Near. A red-eyed, unshaven exquisite appeared in Augustus's state room, took some breakfast, and announced that the yacht was carrying the Prince of Wales.

This came as no surprise to Augustus, who after thirty-odd years of dealing with the Duchy was closely attuned to the

OPPOSITE PAGE TOP Hell Bay and Castle Bryher with the Bishop lurking in the haze. The subject matter of this painting can now be seen more or less unchanged from the Hell Bay Hotel.

OPPOSITE PAGE BOTTOM The principal entrance to Tresco Abbey from Carn Near, where the Prince landed. Mr Smith's taste for cyclopean masonry is well illustrated by the gable wall, which seems to grow out of a granite outcrop, so it is hard to tell where the one begins and the other leaves off. The woman crossing the bridge is heading for Augustus Smith's billiard room, built separately from the house so the cries of the revellers would not disturb more sedate house guests.

disturbances it made in the ether. By half past eleven he was on board the yacht welcoming his landlord, agreeably surprised that Prince Albert's autocratic pomposity had not descended to his son. Augustus's reception of the Prince was a glorified version of his usual hospitality to visiting yachtsmen. The Royal yachties had baths, then a scratch lunch of 'water suchet . . . hot lobster, a new dish for all, beans and bacon, prized as a homely one, and the cold pudding as a rarity; so they pretty well made a dinner.' Augustus dined with the Prince that evening, and the Prince later asked for his photograph. It was a convivial meeting between people of different generations. More and more Augustus Smith appeared to the younger generation as a wild but benevolent uncle.

About now, a true nephew came to visit him. This was Thomas Algernon Smith-Dorrien, son of his brother Algernon and Mary Ann Smith-Dorrien, née Drever, she of the implacable boycott on moral grounds. Thomas Algernon was by now a nineteen-year-old cavalry officer, who considered that Augustus's affairs were his own affair. He was not afraid to defy his mother, and inclined – happily, as it turned out later – to be seduced by the landscape and amenities of Scilly.

It was a busy summer of house parties and island administration. Augustus had no Parliament to return to, but in October he headed up country again, to visit his Parliamentary friends. Perhaps through contact with still-sitting MPs, a sort of yen for public life returned. As autumn gales blew the roof off his new state room and felled a third of the trees on the Abbey Hill, he mulled over schemes to undo Captain Vivian, his fellow Truro Liberal, instigator of much dirty work at the political crossroads.

Truro was impossible. Besides, there was other politics on

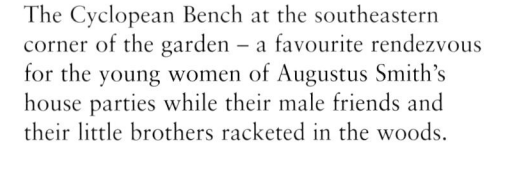

The Cyclopean Bench at the southeastern corner of the garden – a favourite rendezvous for the young women of Augustus Smith's house parties while their male friends and their little brothers racketed in the woods.

his mind, infinitely more delicate than the Westminster model. Sir William Hooker of Kew had died early in 1865, and Augustus had lost no time in reopening communications with his son and successor, Joseph. Joseph (later Sir Joseph) was less ferociously territorial than his father, and more inclined to recognize the value of Augustus's garden, already becoming known as 'Kew with the lid off'. Soon, seeds and cuttings began to flow in both directions, and the relationship between the two great collections has never looked back. Augustus was also in vigorous communication with Lord Ilchester, owner of the sea-warmed garden at Abbotsbury. He was also, through his own and Lady Sophia's travels, casting his net over nurseries in the Channel Islands (which he found a suburbanised version of Scilly) and Belgium. His enlightened education policies on Scilly were also bearing garden fruit, with the inflow of plants from Australia, California and South America via merchant officers who had received their grounding in navigation in Scilly schools. Excursionists, arriving by the now reliable steam packets, flocked to see these botanical marvels. A lesser man than Augustus Smith might have succumbed to a justifiable complacency.

Shipman's Head in a northwesterly gale. The pilot cutter is entering the Tresco channel under a minimum of sail – a tiny rag of jib, and the luff of the triple-reefed mainsail hauled up with the tricing line.

MIGHT VERSUS RIGHT.

Navigator. "WHAT'S THAT YOU SAY?"
Policeman. "WHY, I'LL TAKE YOU TO THE STATION HOUSE, IF YOU DON'T MOVE ON."
Navigator. "YOU TAKE ME TO THE STATION-HOUSE? TEN ON YOU MIGHT!",

ABOVE The avengers of Berkhamstead Common were navvies, Herculean diggers of canals, and builders of railways – a roofless tribe of enormous stature and bottomless thirst, terrifying to the public, loyal to their gangmasters, paying no attention to the law of the land.

OPPOSITE PAGE TOP Tresco Abbey from the south. The original part of the house is visible on the right.

OPPOSITE PAGE BOTTOM Augustus Smith at work in his drawing room. He is sitting in what was originally the verandah, now glassed in. On his desk and the tops of the bookcase are specimen vases containing flowers currently out in the garden. By his left hand are his binoculars, and by his right a basket bearing the piles of letters, accounts public and private, and legal and parliamentary papers, through which he daily worked his way. His dog Yappy is at his feet.

But this would have been quite out of character. Quietness was for Augustus a chance to listen for the sound of distant battle, and having heard it, to start marching towards the guns. A fair-sized battle was at hand, and a famous one, because fought not in islands hiding over the western horizon, but on the doorstep of London.

It concerned Berkhamstead Common. The chinless Lord Brownlow had decided to enclose this expanse of common land in the name of agricultural improvement. To Augustus and other holders of rights on the common, this was cover for a vulgar land-grab by an autocrat. In February 1866, Lord Brownlow's men enclosed 600 acres of the common with 'strong, high iron railings.' Augustus was not amused. 'When [Lord Brownlow] bought the Berkhamstead estate of the Duchy he must have bought their shabby, tricky ways, for which he may depend upon it he will suffer like the Duchy in the long run,' he boomed. Anticipating a legal attack, Lord Brownlow alerted his solicitors. But Lord Brownlow was an inhabitant of genteel Berkhamstead. He had forgotten (or did not have the wit to deduce) that Augustus Smith's time at Scilly had accustomed him to deal with the physical violence of the Atlantic in a highly physical way.

So while the Brownlow lawyers twisted their assertions into arguments, Augustus hired 120 navvies, filled them up with gin and beer, loaded them onto a special train, and despatched them to Tring at dead of night. From Tring they marched through the dark to Berkhamstead. At Berkhamstead they prised Lord Brownlow's fence out of the ground, rolled it into a series of large balls, and left it where His Lordship would see it from his breakfast room window.

His Lordship gibbered with rage, and commenced spewing writs. Britain was delighted. A long and highly satisfactory parody of Macaulay's 'Horatius on the Bridge' appeared in *Punch*:

Augustus Smith of Piper's Hole
By Piper's Hole he swore
That the proud Lord of Brownlow
Should keep the waste no more . . .

In an atmosphere of imminent Reform Bills – the second Reform Act, doubling the franchise, was to appear next year – Augustus had suddenly become a champion of popular justice. He was, in the words of a common-land historian, 'a man entirely without deference, save for the equity of the Common

82

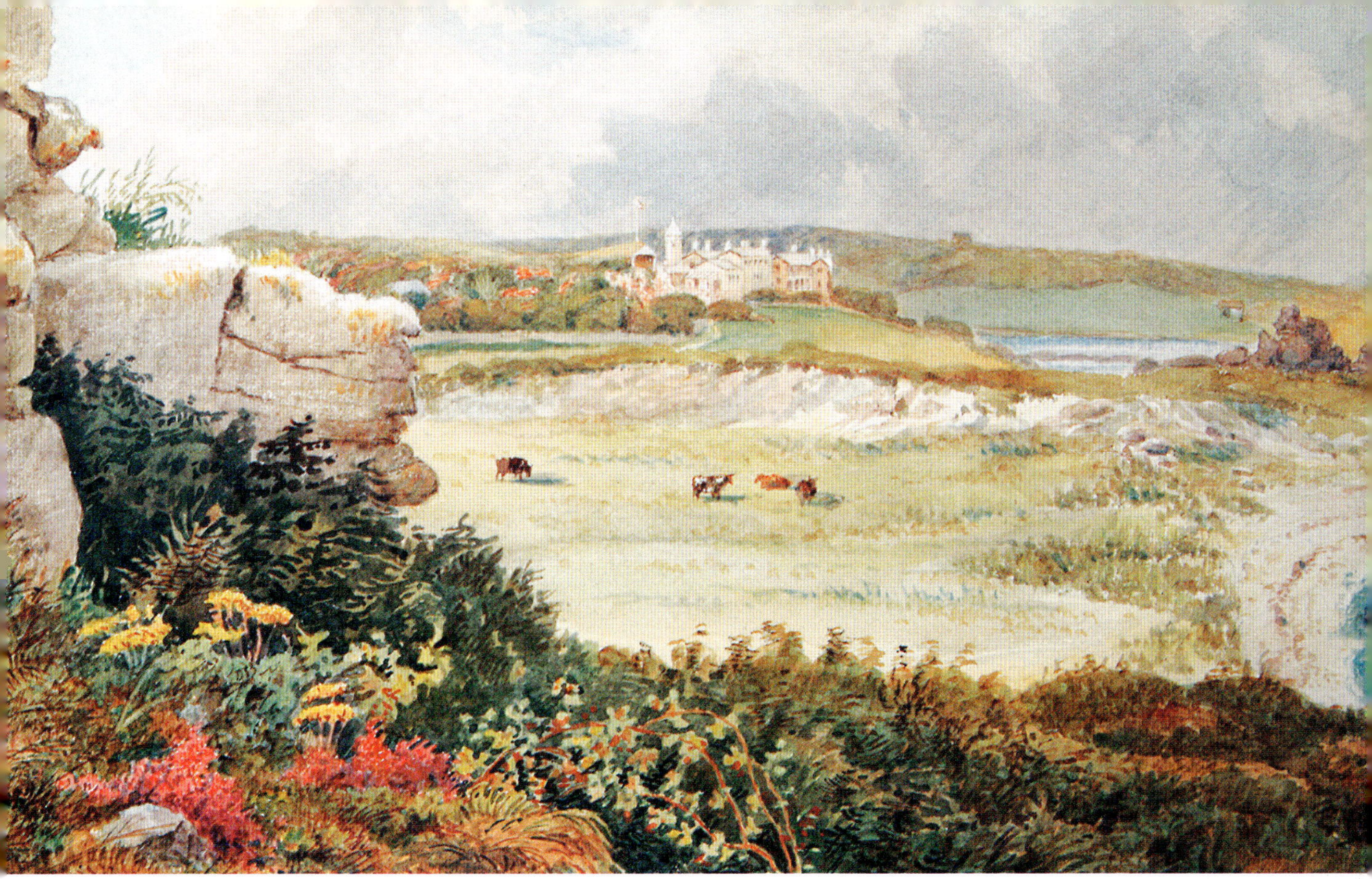

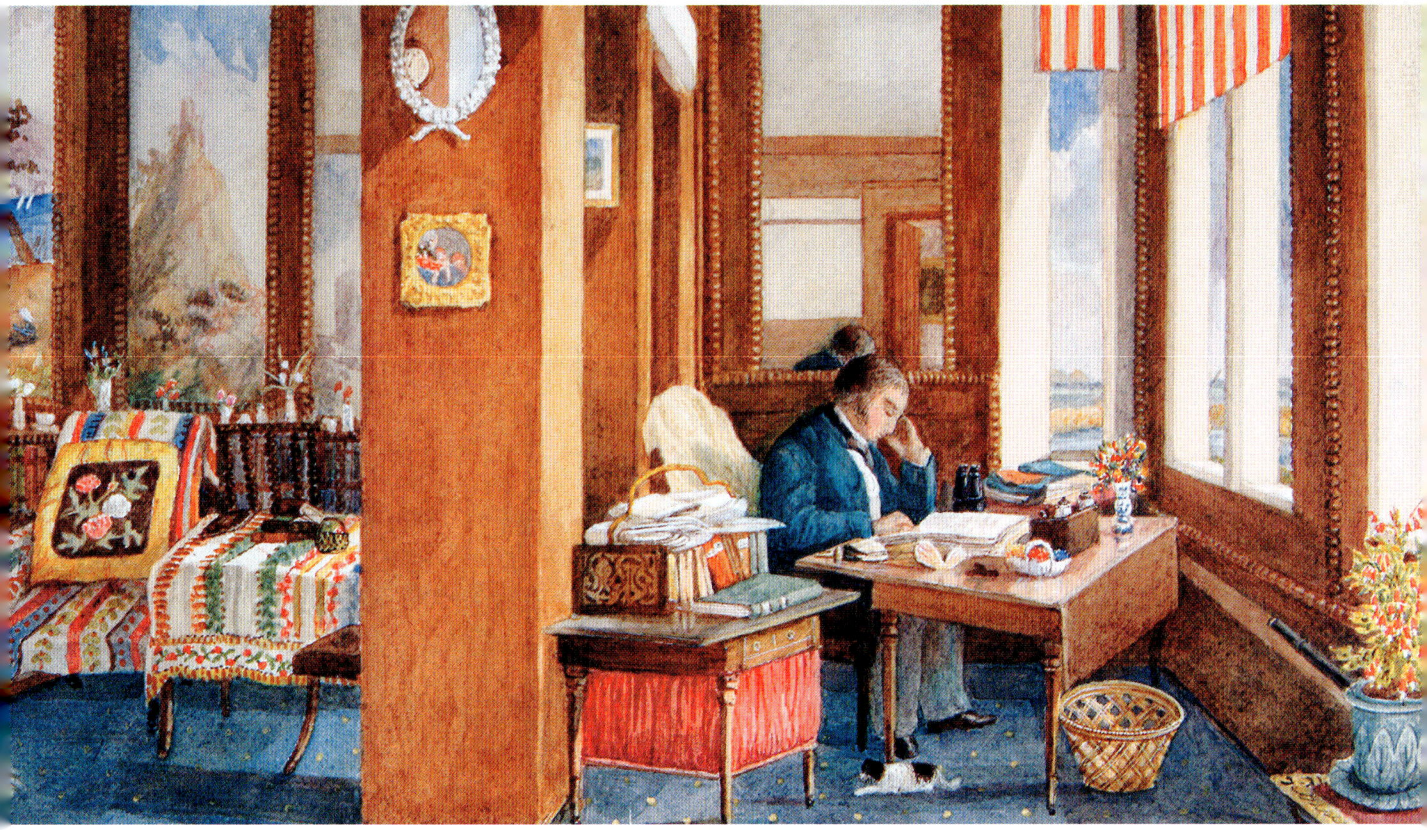

Yappy, a small dog loved by its owner and toughened up by day-to-day contact with dachshunds.

Augustus Smith by his Puyas again. He has become somewhat rotund; but then everything has grown, including (to his evident satisfaction) his garden.

Law, and having seen off the [Duchy of Cornwall] he did not rate highly the challenge of a mere Peer of the Realm.'

Writing from St Michael's Mount, home of giants and St Aubyns, Augustus said: 'I had certainly no idea my necessary practical work would make such a sensation, which has extended to these regions.' This is certainly disingenuous, if forgivable. There was nothing he loved more than to tease the over-mighty, and the mass outpouring of popular acclaim was a new and delightful experience.

Not that he was universally popular. Memories in Cornwall are long, and affairs like the eviction of the Bickfords still rankled in some minds. Memories were revived by one of his total failures of tact. Augustus now advocated the removal of the Geological Society from Penzance, whose burghers had raised the funds for its still splendid building, to Truro. Penzance was not impressed, and Augustus resigned from the Society, hurt, offended, and perhaps, as understanding dawned, somewhat guilty.

Despite the glories of the Battle of Berkhamstead Common, it is possible to see signs that his grip was slackening. One of these was his havering about the introduction of the electric telegraph to St Mary's, an introduction that was in his gift as Lord of the Manor. 'The time is not yet ripe,' he said repeatedly, before he finally relented[13].

By the late 1860s, Augustus was no longer a well man. He had put on a great deal of weight. The throat infections that had plagued him throughout his life became increasingly severe and long-lasting. In the autumn of 1867 he meditated going away for the winter 'to get a good sun-warming to make me comfortable for the close of my life.' His sense of responsibility, however, made this impossible. The world was in a state of confusion. The collapse of the bankers Overend and Gurney led to general consternation among the small savers of Scilly, most of whom had their savings at Bolitho's bank in Penzance, and many of whom did not discriminate between one bank and another. Boatloads of Scillonians rowed to Penzance to check that the bank had survived the crash (it

13. The first attempt to lay the cable was not a success. The cable ship misjudged the tide, and ended up five miles south of St Mary's with nothing left on the reel. A few hundred yards were cut off, and the end brought ashore on St Mary's amid music, cheers and cannon fire. Mr Rowlands, the resourceful Welsh engineer, made the necessary connections and spent a suspenseful afternoon sending himself messages of congratulation, to which he replied in the most fulsome terms. The inspectors pronounced themselves satisfied and left. A second, working cable was installed a year later.

had). A Prussian barque foundered off the Eastern Isles, and a Dutchman was found in a sinking condition to the southward. Both were insurance jobs, and confirmed in Augustus Smith the notion that 'the rascality of ship owners seems greatly on the increase.' And worst of all, the Reform Act, which would double the size of the electorate, had become the pole by which the Tory Disraeli – constitutionally opposed to reform – planned to vault to power at the next election. All these events, linked only by their fudge and crookery, excited Augustus's deep scorn and constant vigilance, at the same time as giving him the old man's sense that the world had changed past the point where he had a place in it.

He found some solace in setting the islands once again in order, ferreting out yet more ministers and schoolmasters, and converting the Garrison House on St Mary's into Scilly's first recorded holiday flats – to be 'let, but only to genteel people, and for a period not less than a fortnight.' Up country, Lord Brownlow's lawyers were issuing a storm of writs against him for criminal damage to His Lordship's fence. Only the vaguest of rumblings reached Tresco, dwarfed by the colossal importance of golden orioles nesting in the garden. 'I am growing very lazy and more of a limpet each day,' wrote Augustus to Lady Sophia.

There were occasional trips to Cornwall, long house-parties of up to fifty people, a winter which as usual was the worst in living memory. In February 1868, his friend and mentor Sir Charles Lemon died. 'I feel every year more that I belong to the

A piece of marginalia from a family album. All natural events at Scilly were eagerly recorded by members of his house parties.

Augustus Smith's friends the Dillwyns were South Walian industrialists and social pioneers who visited most summers. Mr Dillwyn had met Mr Smith in Parliament. The young Dillwyns were keen shots. Judging by the kitchen chair, included for scale, this grey seal is something of a record. It may, however, have been a stray Bearded seal; in which case it was still extraordinary, but in range, not size.

Seal shot by H. Dillwyn Esq near Maiden Bower Rock Isles of Scilly Aug 20. 1866

Watercolour painting – the Victorian equivalent of digital photography. Most of the pictures in this book were painted by Fanny le Marchant or Lady Sophia Tower, who considered them not as works of art but as holiday snaps.

sixth form,' said Augustus, 'and if entitled to its privileges, am also liable to its casualties and risk.'

This gloomy mood was dispelled by another 'mesembryanthemum and guinea fowl summer', with visiting yachts and house parties. On September 14 he celebrated his 64th birthday with a party at Huntsmoor, the Towers' house in Hertfordshire, all Towers and Turrets present. He was back at Scilly by October 1, 'the feast of St Pheasant', energised to the point where he was hoping once again to be asked to stand for Parliament. But the Liberal young Turks were in control of the new enlarged Truro electorate, and before Augustus could leave the islands to canvass the electors, his mare had shied at some seals, he had fallen with a crash on a pile of stones, and had been taken to his bed, no bones broken but badly bruised and much shaken. His recovery was slow, and he was never quite the same man again. But even now, on the brink of his final decline, he was capable of battle.

He began by returning to his old theme of lighthouse management. He suggested that the management of seamarks be passed to the coastguard, 'in the present collapsed state of the smuggling industry . . . to give them some occupation besides hoisting what are called "warnings" to fishermen and sea-gulls in the neighbourhood, who generally understand the signs of the weather better than their official instructors.'

From here he passed to a full-blown attack on Trinity House. He had always loathed 'institutions which exist rather for the benefit of the administrative staffs than the objects paraded in the advertising title.' Trinity House was one of these. The pretext for the battle – as usual a good one, with natural justice on his side – was Trinity House's unjust treatment of the Scilly pilots.

Pilotage on Scilly was more a profession than a job. The men who risked their lives to guide ships through the lethal tangle of ledges to the west of the inhabited islands were as skilled as any surgeon. In those days of ships without engines, they held in their minds complex tidal atlases, systems of weather forecasting, and the topology of a maze of rock and channel, most of which was invisible. There were hundreds of marks, or transits: Tresco quay outside Cromwell's Castle clears Pollack rock, the Crow Beacon in line with the Telegraph takes you into Old Grimsby, but watch Half-Tide rock off the Blockhouse. A pilot's mind must hold a complete catalogue of such marks, and interpret them in the light of deeper intuitions that were just as important and could take a lifetime to develop.

Augustus Smith had a great admiration for the profession, and also – as an old man himself – for the accumulated wisdom that age brings. The Elder Brethren of Trinity House did not share this view. They had insisted, against Augustus's principled objections, on ruining the health and character of teenagers by making them lighthouse keepers. Now they introduced the Revised Pilotage System.

Under the System, Trinity House decreed that the number of licensed pilots on Scilly be reduced to eighteen, and that the upper age limit for a pilot be set at thirty. Eighteen was well below the minimum number of pilots needed. Furthermore (held Augustus) at the age of thirty a pilot would only just be entering a maturity of experience and judgement that made

Resupplying the Bishop Rock Lighthouse, on a relatively calm day. This post-Augustus Smith photograph gives some idea of the difficulty of the process. The boat is moored to a buoy, and the supplies are going up by breeches buoy. In rough weather – and around the Bishop rough weather is more the rule than the exception – resupply becomes difficult, and the exchange of keepers impossible. In early days, the Bishop was the scene of some of Europe's last cases of scurvy.

Augustus Smith and the St Agnes pilots. The man on his right may be his agent. The others, active and superannuated, have faces that can still be found on Agnes today.

him a steady and useful citizen, as sheaves of testimonials from grateful ships' masters would bear witness.

Trinity House, adopting a familiar tactic when faced with questions for which it had no answers, ignored Augustus. They ceased payment of pensions to ex-pilots caught helping out licensed pilots – this even though the assistance was necessary, and the pensions were funded by contributions levied on the ex-pilots during their time of employment. It was a grotesque act of injustice by an autocratic body. Naturally, Augustus responded.

He published another of his celebrated 'Memorials', this time for the attention of the Board of Trade, outlining the facts and engaging in a forensic dissection of the Trinity House accounts. This enabled him to point out that Trinity House spent an iniquitously high proportion of its yearly income on the building and maintenance of the luxury yachts in which the Elder Brethren made their tours of inspection. Trinity House responded with a broadside of mud aimed at Augustus's morals and integrity. But if Augustus had one virtue it was integrity, so none of the mud stuck. He was indeed able to point out that the chief libeller, a Captain Owen, had towed the wrecked barque *Oriental* as far as Penzance, changed his mind, towed her back to Lamorna, and allowed her to break up in such a place that her useful debris and valuable cargo had ended up in his front garden. Augustus was at a loss to understand why this should have been. Either it was the result of the blackest corruption, or spectacular incompetence. Obviously (suggested Augustus, all innocence) corruption was out of the question. Which left only one alternative . . .

Captain Owen at this point went mad with rage and perjured himself all over the *Cornish Herald*. In an uncharacteristic flash of shrewdness and to Augustus's lasting regret, he did not sue Augustus for libel. Trinity House went quiet. But it was not the quietness of defeat, and Augustus knew it. Trinity House was four hundred years old, and Augustus was only one man, sixty-five and far from well. Trinity House could afford to wait, and they would not have to wait long.

At Christmas 1870 the islands were white with snow against an ink-black sky and sea. There had been gales. A French barque had gone ashore at Portloo, an English timber ship on Tean, another timber ship at Carn Near. Scilly had returned to

The wreck of the *Minnehaha* in 1874. This photograph, taken after Augustus Smith's death, is a shocking illustration of the possible consequences of a pilot shortage at Scilly.

ABOVE A busy harbour, a thriving hotel, a prosperous island. In Augustus' day, the harbour would have been St Mary's, the hotel Tregarthen's. This is Old Grimsby on Tresco, and the hotel is the Island, which has grown up in the landscape painted in the watercolour on page 23 – branches springing from roots planted by Emperor Smith.

OPPOSITE PAGE Looking towards Carn Near in 1870. Mats of mesembryanthemum stream down the left-hand wall, cordylines rise above the agaves on the right of the path, and a large proportion of the German merchant fleet lies in the roads, sitting out the Franco-Prussian war.

an atavistic ferment of 'wreck, wreck, wreck, as if everyone was going to make his fortune.' Augustus did not enjoy this chaotic state of mind. And in the middle of the frenzy, his horse shied at one rock, jumped over another, and deposited him with a crash on the ground.

This time it was his shoulder that bore the brunt, and the pain never really left him. As he recovered, the Prussians went to war with the French. Augustus thought both sides were unspeakable. St Mary's Roads filled with Prussian ships reluctant to run the French gauntlet in the Channel. His sister Fanny le Marchant and a large and ever-changing house party frolicked on Scilly's beaches and thronged the Abbey's state rooms. Augustus, a kindly, booming presence, kept mainly to his desk, and moved slowly if at all.

Much of his work was to do with the running of his islands. But it was only now that the garden achieved its final form. If anyone had accused Augustus Smith of being an artist, he would no doubt have been properly indignant. But in the layout of his garden, the originality of spirit that had brought

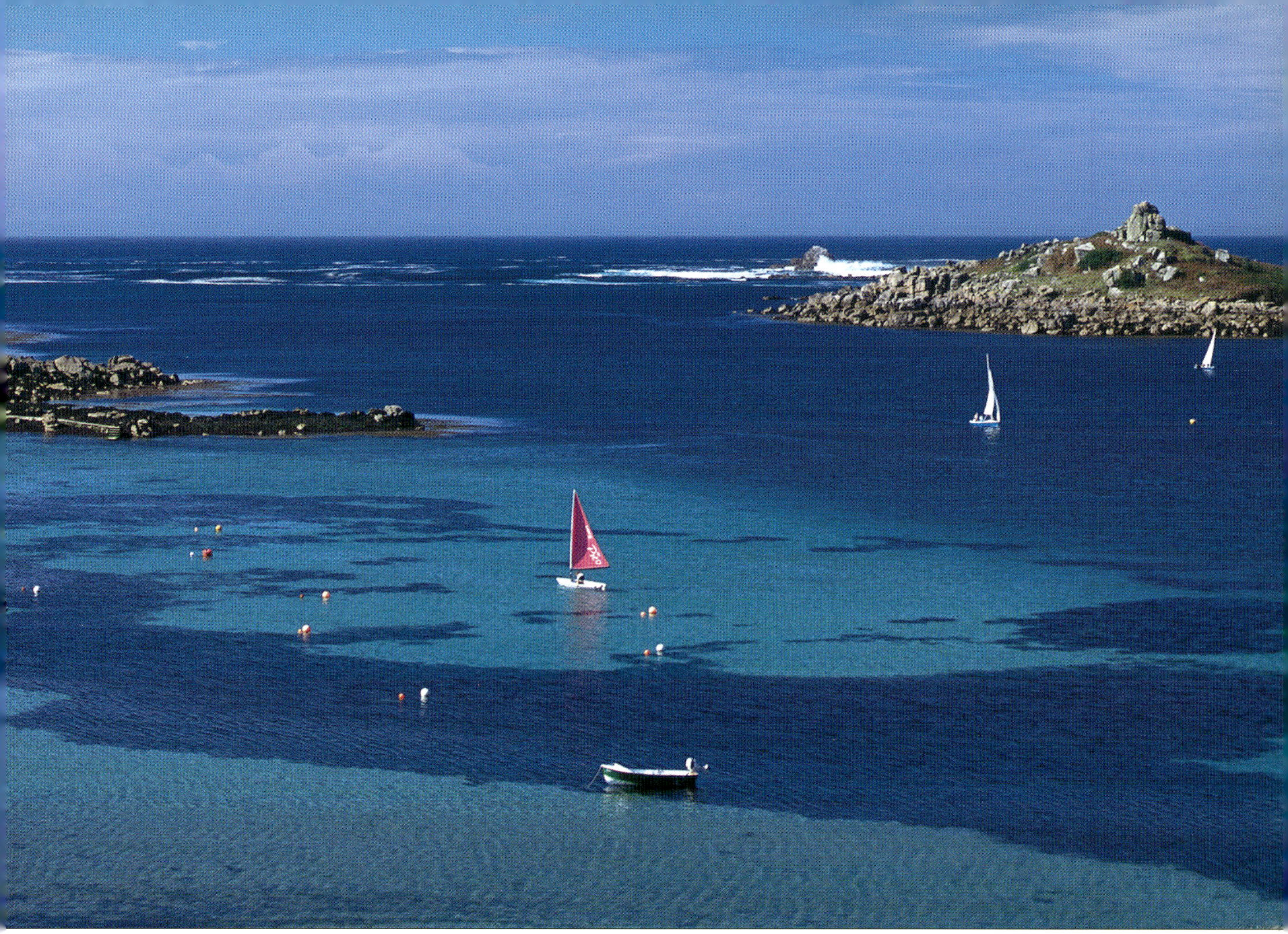

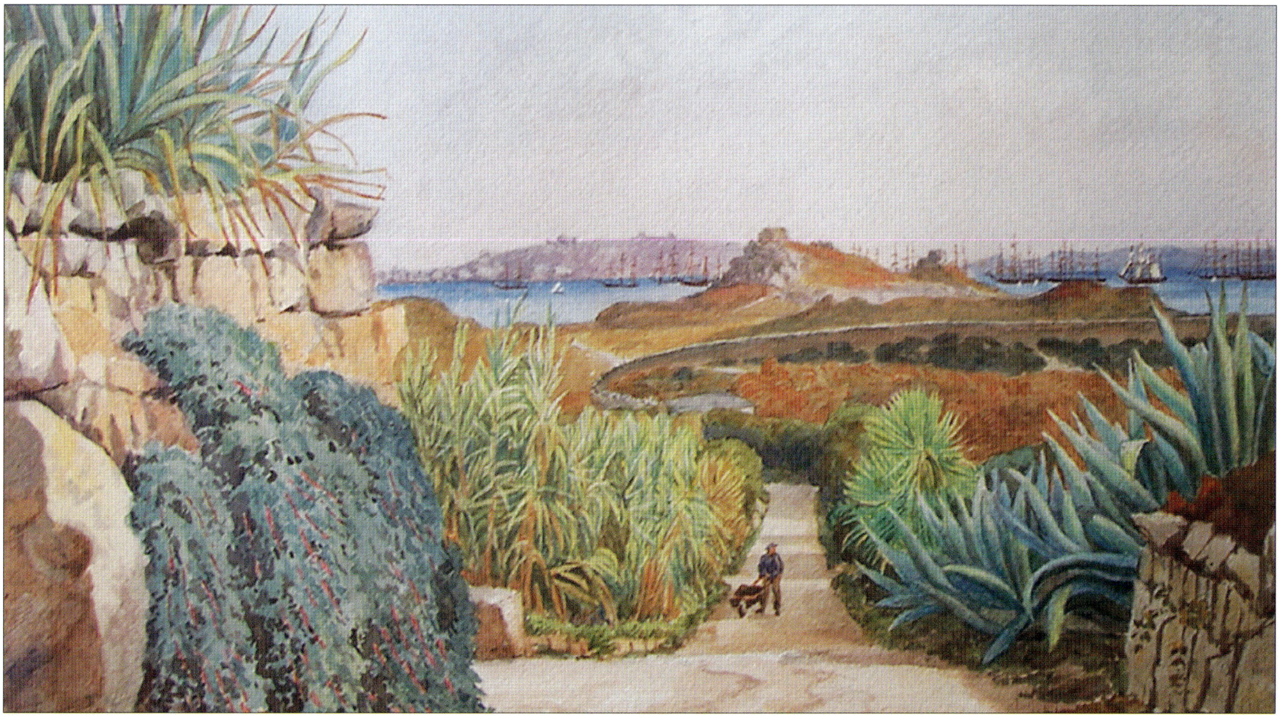

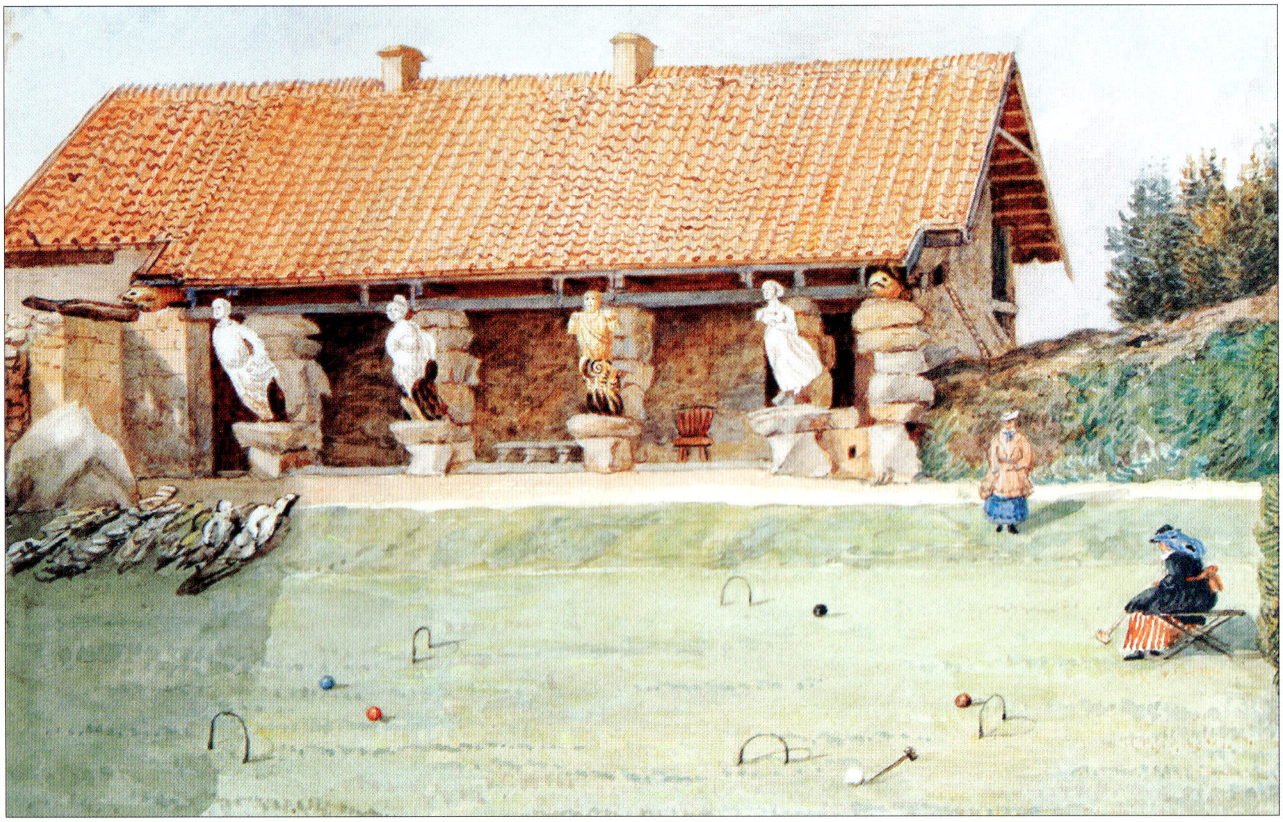

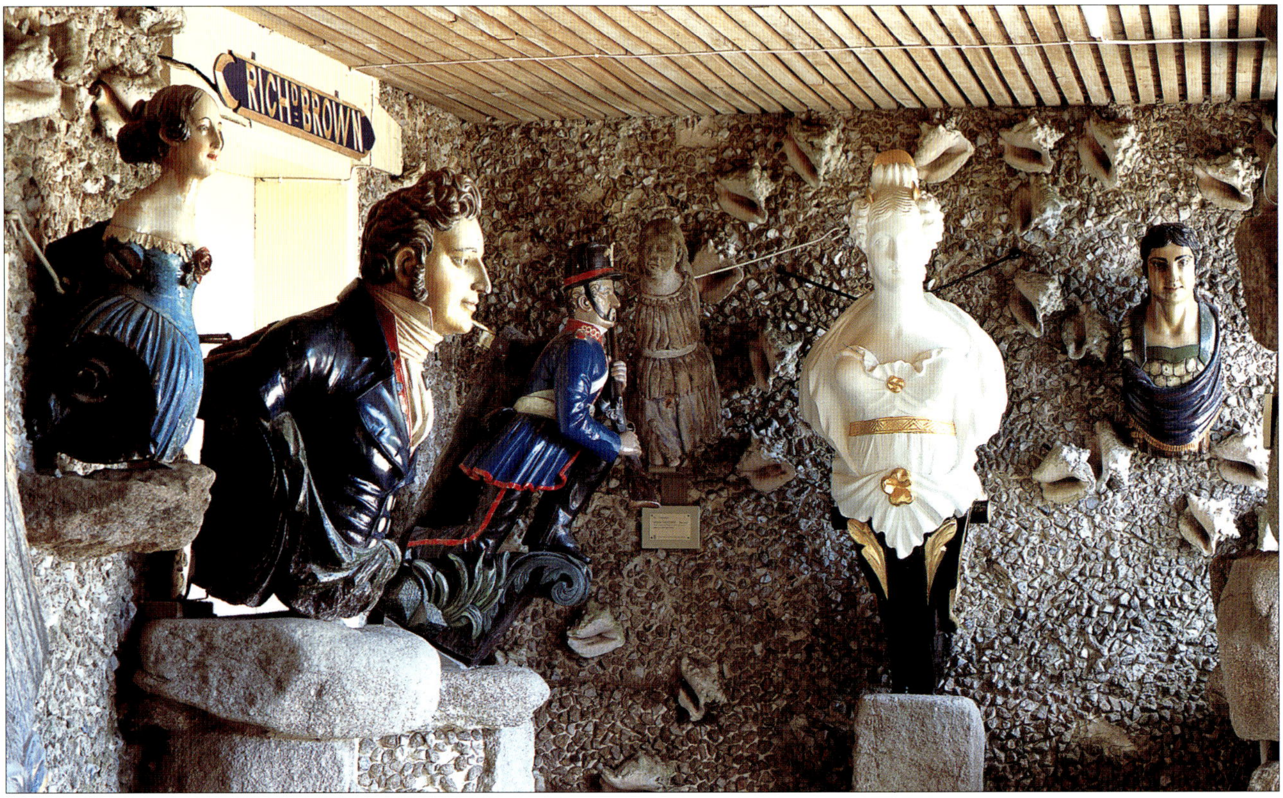
RICHD BROWN

him to Scilly and made it his Lilliput took on narrative form. Bizarrely, the final touch was supplied by a Prussian ship, homeward bound from the Pacific in St Mary's Roads.

From this ship Augustus bought two tons of giant clam, conch and turtle shells. These he bestowed in the shadowy loggia at Valhalla, in front of which he had just constructed the only smooth green lawn in his garden. The picture was complete.

On the top terrace was the kingdom of gods, where Neptune presided over his grand staircase, with a view of the blue heave of the Western seas. In the middle terraces, Australia and Mexico and the Pebble Garden (once planted as a Union Jack) made up the kingdom of men. And down in the green shadows

OPPOSITE PAGE TOP Valhalla shortly after the completion of the croquet lawn.

OPPOSITE PAGE BOTTOM In the loggia at Valhalla. It is now owned by the National Maritime Museum, so it is tidier than in the days of Augustus Smith. But the figureheads still miss their ships, smashed to flinders on Scilly's rocks; and the conch shells Mr Smith bought from the German merchant seamen still contain echoes of Davy Jones.

BELOW The new garden entrance, built in 2003-4. Augustus Smith would undoubtedly have approved. He liked his garden vistas framed, whether by ilex hedges, flowering agaves, or the Abbey Arch itself.

Fanny le Marchant, 'Aunt Fanny' – Augustus Smith's sister, botanical illustrator, watercolourist, chronicler of Scilly, and his lifelong friend.

The *Earl of Arran*, Scilly's steam packet, wrecked in the summer of 1872 as Augustus Smith lay dying. 'Here I am,' he wrote to Lady Sophia Tower, 'regularly laid up on my beam ends and quite as bad as to prospects as the Earl of Arran'.

of the lower garden was Valhalla, the kingdom of the drowned, littered with green bronze cannon, battered figureheads and the empty shells of giant sea-creatures. It was not so much a garden as a universe.

The summer's work came at a price. The writing of his letters to Hooker of Kew was noticeably more crabbed. He took a distant interest in the system of a Mr Fountaine at Chiswick, who had mounted fruit trees on a loop of railway on which they travelled perpetually, receiving all-round doses of light and air. In the summer of 1871, he described himself as an 'elderly gentleman', intending to play slow games of bowls and croquet on his new lawn at Valhalla. But in July, after a flat calm passage to Penzance, he had a stroke that paralysed his right side and slurred his speech, and scuppered yet another plan for a return to Truro politics.

The winter of 1871 was yet again the worst in living memory. The wreck of the *Delaware* provided tough Scillonians with plenty of lace and silk hankies. The two survivors, who had been told that Scilly was staffed exclusively by cannibals, defended themselves with rocks against the brave Bryher boatmen who came to their rescue. Smith could summon up very little irony.

In the spring of 1872 he came again to London, where Lord Brownlow was once again making a nuisance of himself.

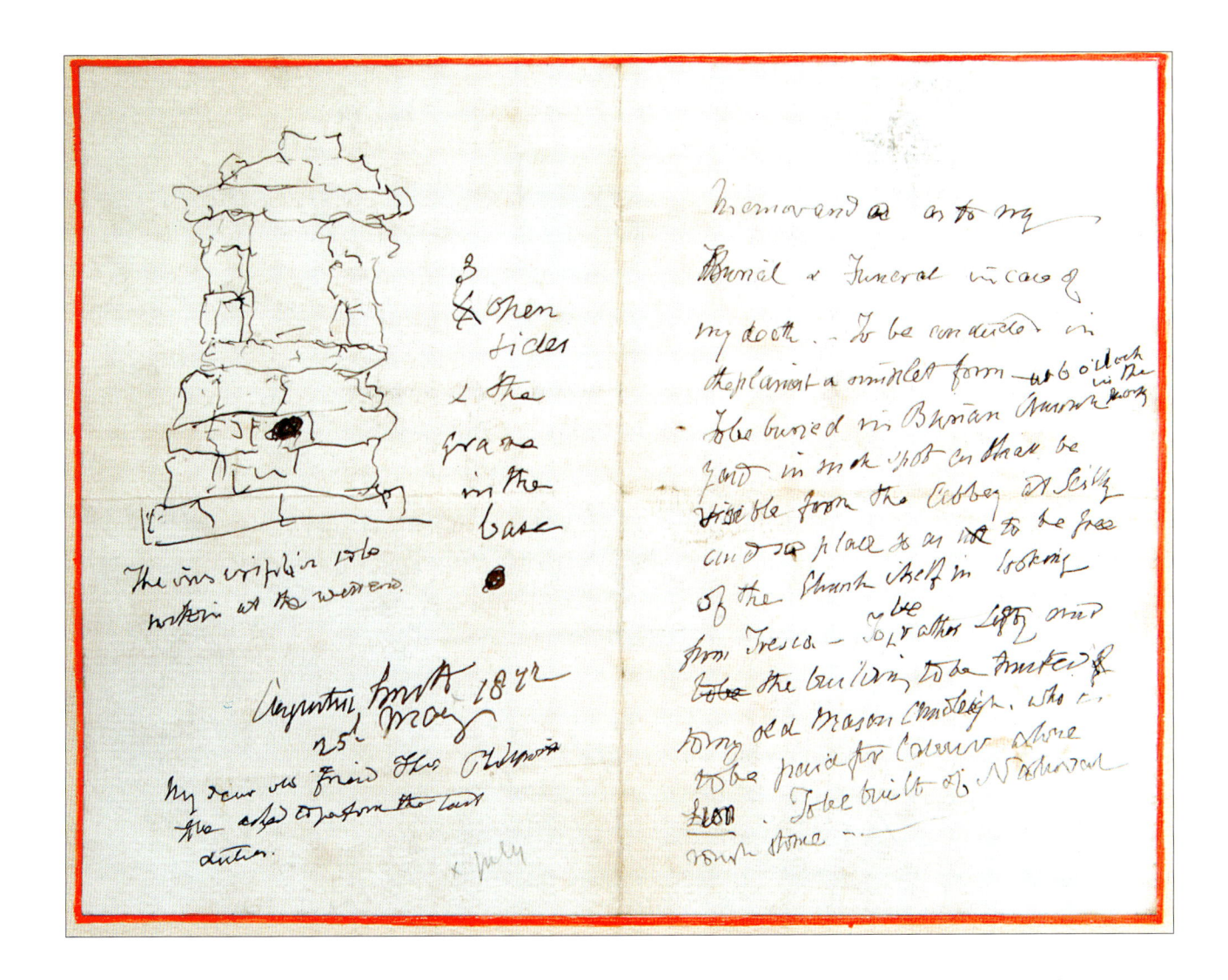

Irritated with the spoilt little Tory lordling who had brought him to the city, he pined for Scilly: 'to sit on a rock and wag my wings, enjoying the sun or shadow of the skies.' In what amounted to a final manifesto, he protested against the need 'to be on guard against the gods of this little earth, who ought to be one's protectors . . . no-one ought to be allowed the privilege of being admitted to the ownership of great estates without proving that they have some sort of acquaintance with the rights and duties contingent upon such possessions.'

In July he headed back for Scilly. He had caught a heavy feverish cold. At a Masonic dinner in St Austell, the cold got the better of him. He had himself conveyed to the Duke of Cornwall Hotel in Plymouth, where he lay gasping for breath. His brother James and sister Fanny rushed to his bedside. He would see them only briefly. He occupied himself with business

Mr Smith's instructions for his funeral and design for his monument. The funeral was 'to be conducted in the plainest and simplest form at 6 o'clock in the morning. To be buried in Burian [sic] church yard in a . . . spot . . . visible from the Abbey at Scilly and so placed as to be free of the Church itself in looking from Tresco . . . the building to be entrusted to my old mason Chudleigh . . . to be built of natural rough stone.' In the event, his instructions were not followed to the letter.

Sunset over Samson.

as the gangrenous congestion spread from his right lung to his left. The only person who came and went as he wanted was William Pendarves, who had for nearly twenty years filled the place of a son in Augustus's life.

On July 19 he wrote to Lady Sophia, who filled part of the place of a wife: 'I am here, at least, for a week longer.' He never left. At one o'clock in the morning of July 31st, in a room in a hotel far from his beloved islands, Augustus Smith breathed his last.

SIX

The Emperor at Rest

AUGUSTUS SMITH had in his life much disliked fuss and pomp. His wishes for the disposal of his body and estate continued this tendency beyond the grave. He stipulated a funeral not on Scilly but in the churchyard at St Buryan, whose tower is the great landmark of the Penwith – visible from the Lizard, and most of all on a clear day from the east windows of the Abbey, a slim menhir beyond the white arrow of the Penzance Road.

The choice of St Buryan seems unaccountable. There is an unproven theory – one of the many that came to surround Augustus in life and after his death – that he had been disgusted by the idea of spending eternity in soil whose freeholder was the perfidious Duchy. There is another, perhaps more plausible, that like his philosophical mentor Bentham he despised pompous obsequies and nodding plumes, and regarded burial less as a religious rite than a hygienic precaution.

To avoid fuss he had stipulated that he should be buried at the unfashionable hour of 6 a.m. His wish for a quiet funeral was not, however, granted. As the sun came up over the land, the sea was seen to be covered with boatloads of Scillonians, tenants and boatmen and pilots and dignitaries, swarming towards the tower that stood black against the bright morning sky. There were massed mayors and masons and landowners and educators and constituents, led by Augustus's old friend John St Aubyn, MP. There were column yards of obituaries in

Augustus Smith chose to be buried not on Scilly, but in the shadow of St Buryan church tower – which on clear days can be seen from Tresco Abbey. His tomb is just visible at the foot of the tower.

Augustus Smith's Monument on Tresco. It now bears the names of the heads of three succeeding generations of his family, which still carries on the work he began at Scilly.

the national and local papers. A polite marble obelisk was erected in the burying ground at the Old Church on St Mary's. And a monument of cyclopean masonry – a fine, barbarous object after Augustus's own heart – still stands on the southwestern corner of Tresco, with a panoptic view of the islands.

His will was another memorial. There were legacies to servants and friends. Mary Pender and his children were handsomely provided for, and the superannuated pilots – still without pensions thanks to the spite of Trinity House – found their incomes reinstated through Augustus Smith's munificence. His quarryman was left an income for life, and (a truly Smithian note) trustees to make sure he did not spend it all on drink. It was reckoned that Augustus had spent some two-thirds of his fortune on the islands without expectation of

Tresco Abbey today – begun by Augustus Smith, extended by successive generations.

recovery – a gigantic sum, equivalent to millions today.

There are two Smith mottoes. One is 'Preigne haleine, tire fort' – 'take a deep breath, and hit hard.' The other is 'sic vos, non vobis.' This is a Virgilian tag. It translates as 'so you work, but not for yourself.' Augustus Smith had lived up to both these mottoes to the hilt.

Even from beyond the grave, he made his scorn for the Duchy clear. In the event of no heir accepting the islands – and they were by no means an unmixed blessing – the lease was to be offered back to the Duchy. In the first will, the Duchy was to pay £12000, and £3000 a year thereafter for the remaining period of the lease. In a codicil, not to be opened until the first deal had been rejected, the initial sum rose to £15,000, the offer to remain open for a year after his death. A further codicil, to come into effect on the Duchy's rejection of the previous one, raised the fine to £20,000.

The Duchy did its best to ignore this ingenious tease. Eventually, it was let off the hook by Augustus's nephew Thomas Algernon Dorrien Smith, who married the daughter of Lady Sophia Tower, who persuaded him against commercial logic to take on the Lord Proprietorship of Scilly. The family has played a huge part in the development of Scilly's economy and society ever since.

* * *

When Augustus Smith had first embarked for Scilly, the sky to the west had been dark and empty. Now, the watcher looking west from the cliffs by St Buryan sees the same great darkness sewn with stars. But out there over the horizon the lighthouse beams sweep the sky, and on a clear night there is a faint but homely loom of island lights where once there was only darkness.

In darkness, people can dream. It is the greatness of Augustus Smith that he did dream, and made the dream come true, and in so doing made it possible for the men and women of Scilly – islanders and visitors – to fulfil dreams of their own.

Tresco seen from St Mary's in the early 1870s. All the old landmarks are here: King Charles' Castle on its Downs, the farm, the abbey with its flagpole. But a new landmark stands on the hilltop to the west of the abbey: the monument to Augustus Smith, Lord Proprietor, the man who built Scilly.

Acknowledgements

This book would never have been written without the generous assistance of Robert and Lucy Dorrien Smith, who are carrying on the work that Augustus Smith started. Nor would it have been possible without the unstinting help given by Amanda Martin, the generous and erudite Curator of the Isles of Scilly Museum on St Mary's, in unearthing unpublished Augustus Smith material and gently guiding me away from important solecisms. I must also acknowledge the work of Elizabeth Inglis-Jones and Molly Mortimer, whose lives of Augustus Smith mine deep seams of scholarship.

Thanks are also due to Roy and Eve Cooper of Tresco, Mike Nelhams, Curator of Tresco Abbey Gardens, Henry Birch of Tresco, Jo Edwards, the Library at the Royal Botanic Gardens, Kew, the Royal Cornwall Museum, the Eden Project, Sandra Kyne and Maggie Young.

I must also thank Alex Ramsay for his beautiful original photography, George and Loveday Llewellyn for the early picture of Penzance, Michael Browning and the Berkhamstead Local History and Museum Society for the picture of Ashlyns, Vaughan Ives for the modern photograph of the Abbey on the back cover, Simon Dorrell for drawing the Augustus Smith monogram that appears on page 4, James Long for the photograph of St Buryan church, and Gibson Kyne of St Mary's for the map on page 7 and for the early photographs from the Gibson Collection.

Apart from the early picture of Penzance on page 10, all the watercolours, paintings and drawings are taken from the Tresco Abbey Archive, copyright © R.A. Dorrien Smith, and cannot be reproduced without permission.

Finally, I should like to acknowledge my debt to my great-great aunt Fanny le Marchant and my great-great-grandmother Lady Sophia Tower, without whose casual brilliance with the water-colour brush the history of nineteenth century Scilly would have remained opaque.

SAM LLEWELLYN